WHALES

and other Marine Mammals of

ATLANTIC
CANADA

Tamara Eder
Ian Sheldon

Lone Pine Publishing

Lone Pine Publishing
2311–96 Street NW
Edmonton, AB T6N 1G3
Canada
Website: www.lonepinepublishing.com

Library and Archives Canada Cataloguing in Publication

Eder, Tamara, 1974-
   Whales and other marine mammals of Atlantic Canada / Tamara Eder.

Includes index.

ISBN 978-1-55105-882-5

   1. Whales--Atlantic Provinces—Identification. 2. Whales—Atlantic Coast (Canada)—Identification. 3. Marine mammals—Atlantic Provinces—Identification. 4. Marine mammals—Atlantic Coast (Canada)—Identification. I. Title.

QL737.C4E23 2013   599.509715   C2011-905189-3

Editorial Director: Nancy Foulds
Project Editor: Sheila Quinlan
Production Manager: Gene Longson
Layout and Production: Janina Kürschner
Cover Design: Gerry Dotto
Cartography: Tamara Eder, Janina Kürschner

Illustrations: All illustrations are by Ian Sheldon except: True's Beaked Whale (p. 114), Grey Seal (p. 138), Harp Seal (p. 140), Hooded Seal (p. 146) by George Penetrante; and Harbour Seal (p. 130), Northern River Otter (pp. 125, 148) by Gary Ross.

Photography: Ken Balcomb (p. 104); Angela Buch/Dreamstime.com (p. 74); Renee DeMartin/West Stock (pp. 43, 62, 100, 132); Francois Gohier/ardea.com (p. 90); Tom and Pat Leeson/Image State (p. 80); NOAA/FLFWC (p. 66); photos.com (pp. 128, 141, 150, 151); Jack Stephens (p. 144); Eric Stoops/Corel Corporation (pp. 50, 56, 86, 122); Kevin Walsh (p. 139); Doc White/ardea.com (p. 136).

We acknowledge the financial support of the Government of Canada through the Canada Book Fund (CBF) for our publishing activities.

PC: 16

Contents

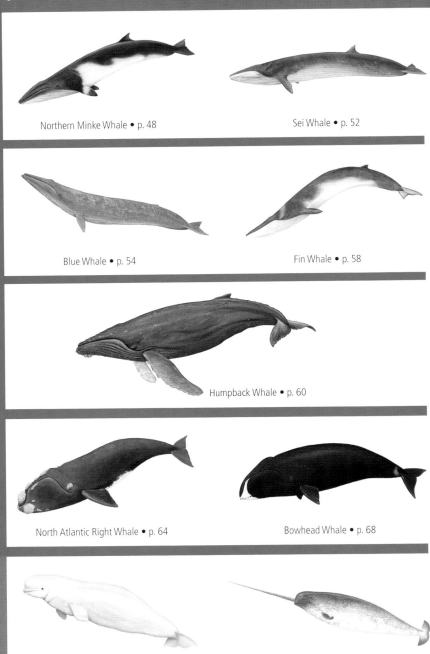

Northern Minke Whale • p. 48

Sei Whale • p. 52

Blue Whale • p. 54

Fin Whale • p. 58

Humpback Whale • p. 60

North Atlantic Right Whale • p. 64

Bowhead Whale • p. 68

Beluga • p. 72

Narwhal • p. 76

BALEEN WHALES

TOOTHED WHALES

TOOTHED WHALES

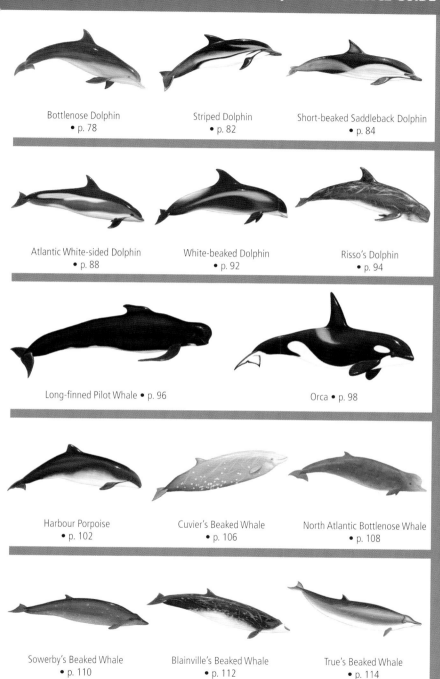

Bottlenose Dolphin
• p. 78

Striped Dolphin
• p. 82

Short-beaked Saddleback Dolphin
• p. 84

Atlantic White-sided Dolphin
• p. 88

White-beaked Dolphin
• p. 92

Risso's Dolphin
• p. 94

Long-finned Pilot Whale • p. 96

Orca • p. 98

Harbour Porpoise
• p. 102

Cuvier's Beaked Whale
• p. 106

North Atlantic Bottlenose Whale
• p. 108

Sowerby's Beaked Whale
• p. 110

Blainville's Beaked Whale
• p. 112

True's Beaked Whale
• p. 114

TOOTHED WHALES

Pygmy Sperm Whale • p. 116   Dwarf Sperm Whale • p. 118

Sperm Whale • p. 120

SEALS AND OTTERS

Walrus • p. 126   Harbour Seal • p. 130

Ringed Seal • p. 134   Grey Seal • p. 138   Harp Seal • p. 140

Bearded Seal • p. 142   Hooded Seal • p. 146   Northern River Otter • p. 148

Introduction

In 1969, we saw Earth from the moon. During the first moon landing, pictures of our planet were radioed back to Earth for everyone to see. These first images of Earth kindled a new kind of enlightenment and shifted our awareness of ourselves and our place on the planet. Seeing images of "Spaceship Earth" sparked two (among many) profound realizations that not only affected our thinking at the time but also would eventually affect the relationship between humans and whales. Primarily, the images reminded us that Earth is dominated by oceans. More than 70 percent of our planet's surface is covered by water, and the creatures that thrive in the marine habitat are marvelous in their form and adaptation. The second realization, rather less obvious, is that we may not be alone in this universe, and we conjured up a keen anticipation of finding non-human intelligence. One result of these combined realizations was a new appreciation for those animals that live in the sea, and when we looked into the eyes of whales and saw something familiar and intelligent, we redoubled our efforts to understand and protect these great creatures.

Whales have fascinated people for thousands of years. At least 3500 years ago, the early Greeks used images of dolphins on mosaics, frescoes, vases and coins. Aristotle is believed to be the first person to propose that whales and dolphins are mammals, not fish, and he correctly identified and classified several different species.

When people speak of whales, they generally imagine the large whales that live in deep oceans. Broadly speaking, the distinction between whales, dolphins and porpoises is based on size rather than zoological affinity: whales are typically the largest of the three, and porpoises are the smallest. Some of the largest dolphins are larger than the smallest whales, however, so the terminology can be confusing. Technically, whales include the Grey Whale, rorquals, Bowhead Whale, right whales, Beluga, Narwhal, sperm whales and beaked whales. Dolphins include the Orca, pilot whales, ocean dolphins and river dolphins. There are only six species of porpoises worldwide.

All whales, dolphins and porpoises are members of the order Cetacea, and they are commonly called "cetaceans." They are distinguished from other mammals by their nearly hairless bodies, paddle-like forelimbs, lack of hindlimbs, fusiform bodies and powerful tail flukes. At least 88 species of cetaceans are known to exist today, and they are scientifically classified into two suborders according to whether they have baleen or teeth. The baleen whales are in the suborder Mysticeti, and the toothed whales are in the suborder Odontoceti. There are only 11 species of baleen whales worldwide: the Grey Whale, rorqual whales, Bowhead Whale and right whales. The toothed whales number at least 70 species worldwide, including the porpoises, dolphins, sperm whales, Narwhal, Beluga and beaked whales.

Whale Origins and Evolution

The evolutionary history of whales is truly remarkable. Mammals originated on land, so cetaceans must have arisen from terrestrial ancestors. In fact, their closest living relatives are the artiodactyls: even-toed hoofed mammals such as cattle, antelopes, pigs and hippopotamuses. Artiodactyls and cetaceans have common ancestors that are unlike either of these present-day groups.

Mammals existed as early as 210 million years ago, but the great dinosaurs dominated the world until 65 million years ago, and mammals remained very small and insignificant. After the dinosaurs died out, mammals had the chance to diversify, and they evolved to walk the earth, fly in the sky and swim in the oceans. The first ancestor of whales known through fossil finds is likely the 50-million-year-old

Ambulocetus, an amphibious, dolphin-sized mammal that had hindlegs with webbed feet for swimming. Ambulocetus probably gave rise to Pakicetus, which still had legs but had a more whale-like skull, teeth, jaw and tail stock. By the early Oligocene epoch (34 million years ago), several toothed whales existed, and Mammalodon, the baleen whale ancestor, also appeared. Once the basic physiology was established, cetaceans diversified dramatically, and by about 7 million years ago, the major forms of whales, dolphins and porpoises that we recognize today had evolved.

separated breathing and eating. The ears were modified for hearing underwater, and echolocation developed in the toothed whales. The dorsal line of the whale adapted to create better propulsion underwater: the neck vertebrae stiffened, a dorsal fin originated, muscles and bones along the tail stock strengthened, and the tail flukes developed. The skull and jaws were highly modified, and the division between baleen and toothed whales occurred. This division was paramount because the baleen whales became specialized for catching large quantities of small creatures, whereas the toothed whales could catch smaller quantities of larger prey. Other modified features common to all whales include a highly streamlined body and a nearly total loss of body hair.

Over millions of years of evolution, the body plan of the whale changed dramatically from that of its four-legged progenitor to the oceanic form we see today. The loss of the hindlimbs and the modification of the forelimbs into flippers with no moving elbows are striking changes to the basic mammalian plan. Whales still retain a vestigial pelvis and femurs because the selective pressure for eliminating such structures is weak. The blowhole originated from the nostrils, which migrated to the top of the head and effectively

Pakicetus

Although whales and dolphins evolved in the oceans, some species now live in fresh water. The river dolphins, which number five species worldwide, inhabit large river systems such as the Amazon, Orinoco, Indus, Ganges and Yangtze. As well, most porpoises can travel freely between fresh and salt water, as can the Beluga. Generally speaking, however, the saltwater whales tire quickly in fresh water because of their reduced buoyancy, and their skin might wrinkle and slough (just like ours does in a bath).

The fact that cetaceans look a bit like sharks is a tribute to convergent evolution. Sharks and cetaceans are not closely related at all, and there are many physiological differences between them. However, a grey-coloured shark and a dolphin, for example, may be difficult to distinguish at first glance. Their similar appearance reflects a desirable body plan for being a successful ocean creature.

Although mammals have many characteristics that differentiate them from other animals, the most obvious differences between whales and sharks are that whales breathe air and nurse their young, whereas sharks have gills and do not nurse their young. The easiest way to distinguish between sharks and whales, however, is to look at their tails: the flukes of a cetacean are horizontal; the tail of a shark is vertical. Many frightened swimmers have thought that an approaching dolphin was a shark, but a shark swimming close to the surface of the water reveals two triangular "fins" above the surface: its dorsal fin and the top of its tail. Dolphins reveal only their dorsal fin.

Shark

Dolphin

Behaviour and Adaptations

Feeding with Baleen

The baleen whales, or mysticetes, are typically the largest of all cetaceans. Of these, the largest are the females. Ironically, these large whales feed on some of the tiniest ocean creatures.

Baleen plates are a remarkable new mammalian adaptation that permits efficient filter-feeding of plankton, tiny crustaceans, small fish and some molluscs from the ocean water. Baleen was once called "whalebone," but it is really not

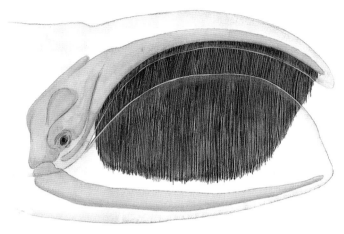

Baleen specialized for skim-feeding (Bowhead Whale)

Baleen specialized for lunge-feeding (Northern Minke Whale)

bone at all. Although baleen grows where teeth normally would on other mammals, it is actually made of an entirely different keratinous material very similar to human fingernails and hair. The baleen plates grow down from the gum of the upper jaw, and they are shaped like very long, narrow triangles. All the plates hang one against the other, similar to vertical blinds on a living room window. The hairs on the edge of each plate face into the mouth.

Lunge-feeding (sometimes known as gulp-feeding), skim-feeding and bottom-feeding are the three basic styles of feeding among baleen whales. Within each style, there is variation between species and even individuals.

Throat distension during lunge-feeding

The rorqual whales primarily use lunge-feeding. If necessary, prior to surface lunging, the whale herds its prey into a tight group near the surface. Once the prey is concentrated, it lunges and opens its mouth to gulp in tons of food-rich water. A rorqual has specialized throat pleats that expand like an accordion and allow the throat to distend in a balloon-like way. These pleats contract automatically as the whale closes its gaping mouth. The mouth is not closed completely, but just enough to permit the baleen to meet the lower jaw and create a sieve. The water is squeezed out through the baleen, while the krill, copepods and other small creatures are trapped inside the mouth against the baleen. Rorquals have short baleen that is continuous around the front of the jaw, making the mouth an effective filter when it is nearly closed.

Humpback Whale bubble-netting

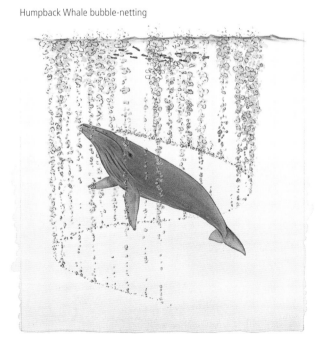

A famous variation of lunge-feeding is bubble-netting, used by Humpback Whales. One or several Humpbacks begin releasing bubbles as they swim in a circle below a school of fish. As the bubbles rise, they create a curtain that disorients the fish and traps them in a central area. Once the fish are concentrated inside this bubble-net, the whales surge up in the middle of the "net" and gulp the creatures into their gaping mouths.

Skim-feeding is passive in comparison to lunge-feeding, and it is a style used primarily by right whales. The Sei Whale, though it is a rorqual, also frequently uses skim-feeding. For a long time, skim-feeding was believed to occur only at or near the surface, simply because we could only see the whales doing it there. Skim-feeding often occurs at great depths, however, and only recently was this activity recorded on film by researchers. This feeding style requires the whale to swim through a school of plankton or other small creatures with its mouth open.

Right whales do not have baleen in the front of their mouths, and the baleen on the sides is very long. When the whale opens its mouth, the opening is like a small cave with walls of baleen. As the whale swims through the food-rich water, the water enters the mouth and continues right out through the baleen. Food also goes into the mouth, but it is trapped by the long baleen. The throat of these whales does not extend, and the mouth is kept still and open as the whale swims. Once many food creatures have accumulated in the mouth, the whale closes its jaws and swallows.

The Grey Whale *(Eschrichtius robustus)*, found only on the west coast, is the only bottom-feeding baleen whale. It feeds by scraping up bottom sediment and filtering out the invertebrates.

North Atlantic Right Whale skim-feeding

13

Feeding with Teeth

The toothed whales feed on creatures larger than those fed on by baleen whales. Their jaws are modified according to their style of feeding and their prey. Dolphins, for example, often have long, narrow jaws that are fast-closing and capable of catching small, darting fish. Orcas have wider jaws with heavy, conical teeth for holding prey and tearing off large chunks. The size of their prey matters little to Orcas, and certain groups of these predators are known to attack other cetaceans, such as porpoises, dolphins and even larger whales and especially their calves. Porpoises have spade-shaped teeth that are flattened side to side. These teeth are effective for slicing and shearing rather than holding prey.

The Sperm Whale and the beaked whales are believed to be suction feeders—by quickly moving the tongue backward in the mouth, they create a powerful suction to pull in their prey—and there is much debate about how useful teeth are to them. The Sperm Whale has a very narrow jaw, relative to the size of its head, with heavy, conical teeth. The white mouth of the Sperm Whale may even act as a lure to bring its prey close. One adult Sperm Whale that was killed had no lower jaw at all—an astonishing injury that appeared to have had little effect on the overall health of the whale, which was large and clearly well fed.

Beaked whales have some of the strangest teeth and jaws of all the odontocetes. Usually, only the male's teeth erupt, and the females feed without any functional teeth. Males have two (or sometimes four) teeth in the lower jaw, either close to the tip of the beak or in the middle. The teeth tend to be large and triangular, and sometimes they overlap the upper jaw on the outside of the mouth.

Orca teeth

Dolphin teeth

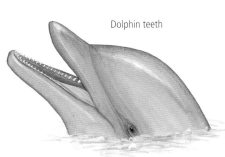

The Blowhole

One of the marvels of cetacean anatomy is the blowhole. Unable to breathe through its mouth, a whale inhales and exhales exclusively through its blowhole. The blowhole is designed for rapid air exchange, and it is the result of an evolutionary change in skull shape and a slow migration of the nostrils and breathing passage to the top of the head—away from the throat. In some cases, most notably the Humpback Whale, air can voluntarily be released from the lungs into the mouth if the trachea is slightly dislodged, but this action does not give the whale the ability to breathe through its mouth.

For whales, breathing is voluntary, and they open and close their blowholes at will. The baleen whales have two blowholes that are controlled by strong muscles attached to the upper jaw. When the whales surface, they make an explosive blow and inhale in such quick succession

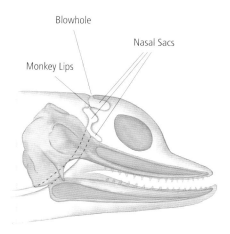

Blowhole

Nasal Sacs

Monkey Lips

that the entire process takes only a few seconds. The toothed whales have only one external blowhole. In fact, they have two nasal passages, each with the ability to open and close, but these passages (called "monkey lips") are hidden internally. The single external blowhole is a new adaptation unique to odontocetes that allows for sound generation by the hidden soft tissues of the nasal passages.

Paired blowholes of baleen whales

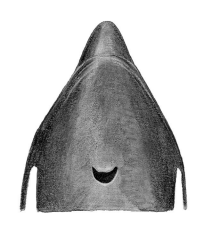

Single blowhole of toothed whales

Sleep

Unlike terrestrial mammals, cetaceans do not enter a deep state of sleep. They must rest, but they require much less sleep than terrestrial mammals. Evidence suggests that whales require less sleep because the marine environment induces a brain state that resembles sleep. Studies show that even humans, when immersed in water for up to six days, may require only one hour of sleep a day instead of the normal eight hours. Moreover, whales are voluntary breathers, so for them to breathe at the surface, to keep moving to prevent stranding and to watch for potential dangers, they must never fall soundly asleep.

To relax, many whales use the technique of "logging" at the surface. Logging is a form of rest where whales float almost motionless at the surface, and if there are two or more, they will all point in the same direction. Their breathing and heart rates are lowered, and their eyes may close, but they have not totally lost consciousness. Mariners once believed that a logging whale was fast asleep and that even an approaching boat could not wake it, but they were mistaken. Dolphins and porpoises are able to "sleep" half their brain at a time.

Lungs and Diving

Perhaps the greatest danger for a deep-diving air breather is nitrogen narcosis, a desensitized state caused by pressurized air entering the circulation system. The other main hazard, the bends, occurs when bubbles spontaneously form in joints and tissues as a result of rising to the surface too fast. Whales are not affected by either of these conditions because of several adaptations that evolved over time.

Before a deep dive, whales remove the air from their lungs. Air is highly compressible, whereas water is not. Like our bodies, most of a whale's body is water and can therefore handle the pressure of a dive. Only the air in the lungs is subject to compression. Any air that remains in a whale's respiratory system is pushed into the inflexible windpipe, where it cannot be compressed. This strategy prevents air compression and thereby effectively

Sperm Whale diving

eliminates nitrogen narcosis. The bends, also known as decompression sickness, is prevented by the efficient and rapid transport of nitrogen back into the lungs as the whale surfaces. Circulation of blood through the muscles during the dive is also reduced, which further reduces the possibility of nitrogen bubbles forming.

Sounds and Songs

In water, sound travels almost five times faster than in air. A cetacean uses sound to keep in touch with other members of its group, and some of the odontocetes use sound for echolocation. Different whales make different sounds, and if the sounds have meaning, one species likely cannot understand another species. Sounds vary from loud to quiet, and from deep rumbles and belches to high squeaks and clicks.

Baleen whales commonly produce the deepest and loudest sounds. The vocalizations of a Blue Whale can be less than 20 hertz in frequency and up to 188 decibels in volume. Sophisticated military technology capable of detecting submarine sounds from far away has been able to pick up the sounds of a Blue Whale from over 2400 kilometres away. This kind of evidence changes how we look at a group of whales. Perhaps whales do not have to be in visual range to be considered part of the same group. Two rorqual whales seen 50 kilometres apart may not be "solo" whales.

Humpback Whales make extremely loud and long songs. Samples of the unique and complex songs of Humpbacks have even been sent out on *Voyager*s 1 and 2, spacecraft that are on their way toward other worlds in this galaxy. The Humpback song samples are in a section of a recording that includes greetings in 55 languages from 60 different countries.

Although Humpbacks are now part of the ambassadorial elite of Earth, no one actually knows how they and other baleen whales produce sound. Baleen whales have a larynx, but they have no vocal cords, and their paired blowholes release no bubbles when they sing. A laryngeal source for the sound is not ruled out, but much more research must be done to determine how mysticete whales make sound.

Blue Whale

In odontocetes, sound production is complex, but it is better understood than sound production in mysticetes. The external blowhole of a toothed whale hides the "monkey lips," or the internal soft tissue of the dual inner nasal passages. The monkey lips can pass air to generate sound, much like we can purse our lips to make squeaking and kissing sounds. One monkey lip can be open while the other is closed, creating a variety of different noises. All the while, the external blowhole stays shut, so no air is released. The sounds made by odontocetes are primarily whistles, squeaks and clicks emitted in a variety of patterns.

Many groups of toothed whales have unique "dialects" different from those of other groups of the same species. All Orcas, for example, produce many similar sounds that are probably understandable from one whale to the next, but closer analysis reveals that one group will produce sound combinations that no other group does. Dolphins also have very sophisticated sounds and sound patterns. Many species have "signature whistles" for each individual, which are probably like human names. Signature whistles are often accompanied by a small string of bubbles released from the blowhole.

Echolocation

The use of echolocation, though it is rare in the animal kingdom, is not unique to whales. Bats, shrews and certain birds are efficient echolocators, and there may be other animals that we are not aware of yet that also use echolocation. Echolocation involves sending out high-frequency pulses or clicks and listening to how these sounds bounce off objects present in the vicinity. Echolocation, particularly the underwater variety, is also known as sonar (SOund Navigation And Ranging). Military organizations once applauded themselves for discovering and using such "advanced" technology. Some of this military pride was shattered upon learning that bats and whales had been doing it for millennia.

As far as we know, only the odontocetes use echolocation. When toothed whales emit the echolocation clicks, the sounds are passed through the "melon"—a specialized structure in their forehead that focuses the

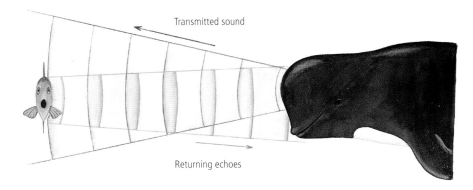

Transmitted sound

Returning echoes

sound. The melon is mainly low-density oil, and it gives toothed whales their distinctive, bulbous forehead. When the outgoing signals hit an object, they bounce back in an altered form. These returning "echoes" are so detailed that the whales can perceive shape, size, texture, distance and probably many more characteristics. The returning signals are received through the lower jaw, which helps transmit the sound to the modified ear.

Echolocation is not limited to surfaces. Evidence indicates that odontocetes can "see" inside things, even inside other bodies, to learn which females (human, dolphin or otherwise) are pregnant. Many interesting research projects involve dolphins and pregnant women; the dolphins seem to be aware of the pregnancy and act differently around these women.

The primary use for echolocation in whales, however, is for finding food and determining their immediate surroundings. The pulses are effective for at least 760 metres, and they allow the whales to hunt even in totally dark or murky water. Some species, such as the Sperm Whale and even the Pantropical Spotted Dolphin, may use such intense pulses that their prey is momentarily stunned, making feeding much easier.

Migration

Both mysticete and odontocete whales may perform migrations of some sort. The baleen whales typically make long migrations between their feeding waters and their calving and mating waters. Most toothed whales are more appropriately called nomadic; their journeys follow food cycles rather than predetermined paths related to certain activities. Sperm Whales, bottlenose whales and Long-finned Pilot Whales make seasonal migrations, but very little is known about the migrations of toothed whales.

In general, and in both hemispheres, baleen whales migrate from high-latitude feeding waters to low-latitude calving and mating waters. The whales often feed only in the high-latitude waters, and during periods of calving, mating and migrating, they consume little or no food. The foods that baleen whales feed on—primarily plankton, krill, copepods and small fish—are particularly abundant in the high-latitude waters. Some theories suggest the baleen whales migrate to warm waters each year because their calves may not be able to survive in the cold though food-rich water, but there is little evidence to support such claims.

The details of why whales migrate may forever remain a mystery to us, as may the mechanics of how they unerringly traverse thousands of kilometres of water. The long journey of migrating baleen whales takes two or three months in each direction. The whales travel nearly constantly at speeds of just a few kilometres per hour. The cues whales use to navigate are not well understood. Perhaps they spy-hop occasionally to follow natural coastal features, or they may be able to detect subtle changes in water "tastes" and currents. Some researchers suggest that whales can use the sun and stars as a compass like we do, or that they may be able to follow sea floor topography. Some cetaceans have the mineral magnetite (iron oxide) present in their bodies, and this is a key substance for biomagnetism (biomagnetism is when an animal can orient itself to the magnetic field of the earth, and perhaps use this ability for travelling long distances). Whichever way they do it, whales continue to dazzle researchers with their ability to travel and accurately navigate over long distances.

Strandings

Strandings are staggering events where whales end up in shallow water and can no longer manoeuvre. If the tide goes out, the whale is left dry on the sand, where it usually dies. Stranding can happen to one whale or to hundreds of whales at a time.

No one seems to know why some cetaceans become stranded. Some people think that in areas of gently sloping beaches, the echolocation of the odontocete whales is distorted. It is true that strandings occur more often with deep-water species, such as Sperm Whales or pilot whales, as if they become disoriented if they get too close to the coastline. Cetaceans that regularly live in coastal waters, such as dolphins and porpoises, rarely strand. In these cases, the individuals that strand are usually injured or diseased. Belugas, which are found in the northern part of our region, may strand when high numbers of them congregate in estuaries and shallow bays (a stranded Beluga will live until the next tide comes to free it as long as a polar bear does not find it). Some Orcas, notably those on Argentina's eastern coast, intentionally strand on rocky beaches where colonies of sea lions are near the water's edge. The Orcas can then grab sea lion pups and wiggle their way back into the water. Likewise, some Bottlenose Dolphins work together to push schools of small fish up onto muddy banks, where the dolphins can easily grab them and then slide back into the water. Other than these examples of intentional stranding, a stranded whale is one whose life is at serious risk.

If you find a whale alive and stranded, do not attempt to touch it or help it. In some countries, it is illegal to help whales unless you have proper training. Unskilled "help" for a stranded whale has often resulted in greater harm to the whale and injuries to the person. The first thing to do in the event of a stranding is to contact the nearest wildlife authorities or the police. If necessary, the immediate first aid for a stranded whale is to make sure its blowhole is unobstructed by sand or debris so it can breathe, and to keep its skin moist so it does not get sunburned or dehydrated.

Long-finned Pilot Whale

Displays and Surface Behaviour

BREACHING: This behaviour is a favourite for whale watchers. A breach is when some or all of the whale's body rises out of the water and splashes back in. Why whales breach is not clear. They may enjoy it, it may help rid the body of barnacles and parasites, or they may do it if they feel insecure or threatened. In some cases, whales breach repeatedly, much to the delight and astonishment of nearby whale watchers. Although many people assume that such instances are positive for both the people and the whale, some researchers suspect that the whale is breaching because of distress from boat harassment. Dolphins may breach in a high leap clear out of the water and spin or somersault while in the air.

LOB-TAILING: A lob-tail is when a whale forcefully slaps its flukes on the surface of the water while its upper body remains submerged. Some species are known to lob-tail as a sign of aggression, whereas others appear to do it for much more benign reasons, such as communication.

SPY-HOPPING: Most whales spy-hop, especially while socializing. Spy-hopping is when a whale raises its head almost vertically out of the water, as if to get a better look around. This may be exactly what it is doing because the whale typically rises only until its eyes are exposed and no more.

FLIPPER-SLAPPING: Cetaceans may occasionally roll onto one side and slap their flippers against the surface of the water. This behaviour may be repeated several times in a row, but we do not understand what it signifies.

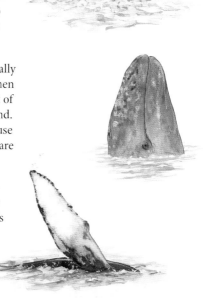

FLUKING: Before a whale dives, it frequently raises its flukes above the surface of the water. For many species, this action indicates that a long, deep dive has started. Researchers may use the markings and scars on the flukes of whales to identify and catalogue individuals.

LOGGING: For most species, one to several whales may "log" at the surface as a form of rest. When several individuals log, they all face the same direction and stay in a close group. Logging requires minimal effort, but it is not an unconscious state because whales must remain at least semi-conscious at all times in order to breathe.

BOW-RIDING: Dolphins, porpoises and some small whales frequently engage in bow-riding and wake-riding. Dolphins appear to enjoy this activity, and people certainly enjoy watching them. The pressure wave created by a moving boat pushes the dolphin along at great speed with minimal energy output by the animal.

PORPOISING: Dolphins and some small whales may break the surface of the water in a low-arcing leap each time they take a breath. This fast mode of travel is called "porpoising," and it is very energy efficient. Air has less resistance than water, and the momentum the cetacean built up underwater propels it a great distance during the leap. In spite of the name, this behaviour is not common among true porpoises.

RUBBING: Rubbing is a behaviour done by several species and is probably to massage the skin or to aid in molting—or simply to feel good. In some regions, Orcas massage themselves on shallow underwater beaches of rounded pebbles, an activity that is sometimes visible to a boater above.

PLAYING: Probably all cetaceans engage in playing activity. Play can be anything and may involve juveniles learning particular behaviours that will aid them as adults. If you see whales or dolphins playing at the surface, enjoy watching them, but try not to disturb their fun or harass them.

BLOWING: One of the first indications that a whale is nearby is the distinct blow it makes upon surfacing. The blow of a whale is visible because of a possible combination of factors. The difference in temperature between the whale's lungs and the outside air, some seawater from the surface of the animal's skin and accumulated droplets of mucous and oils from the whale's lungs and nasal passages all contribute to the blow. The shape and size of the blow varies from species to species. Within a species, blow shape and size also vary. Some species, such as the Sperm Whale, have such unique blows that seeing the blow alone is sufficient to identify the whale. Typically, the first blow after a long dive is louder and bigger than succeeding blows. Blows may be diagnostic of the species when viewed from the front or rear. Side views are usually not as distinct. The blows illustrated below and on the following page are to scale and are all as viewed from the front.

DIVE SEQUENCE: The most frequently observed activity at the surface is the dive sequence. Beginning with a blow, the dive sequence reveals certain characteristics about the animal. The shape of the head and blowhole, the length of the back, the dorsal fin, any dorsal knuckles or bumps, the tail stock and the flukes are all features that may be seen during a dive and that can be diagnostic enough to identify the species.

Northern Minke Whale

Sei Whale

Blue Whale

Fin Whale

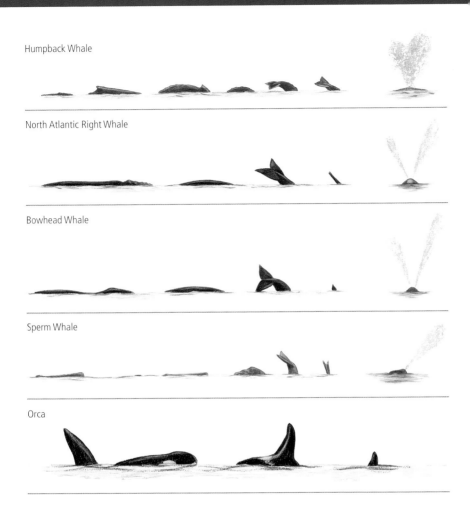

Humpback Whale

North Atlantic Right Whale

Bowhead Whale

Sperm Whale

Orca

Extreme Whales

A simple truth about cetaceans is that many of their characteristics are difficult for us to understand. Their size, their weight, their communication—much of what makes a whale a whale—is unlike anything else we know. Typically, our efforts to understand whales involve compartmentalizing the information so that it is more manageable for us. We like to discuss large whales in terms of minimum and maximum lengths and weights, and we frequently discount reports of overly large whales as either myth or inaccurate reporting.

The framework in which we view whales, however, is not absolute. If the maximum length of a Blue Whale is reported by several authorities to be 30 metres, that does not preclude a whale of 32 metres, or more, from existing. In fact, there is much evidence to support the idea that large whales may keep getting slowly larger the older they get. Whalers of 100 and 200 years ago recorded enormous lengths for many whale species. Because whalers typically took the biggest whales (a simple choice to maximize profit for energy output), they would have taken the oldest whales. Researchers commonly suggest that the reason we do not see such large specimens now is that the whales currently alive are comparatively young. Such a suggestion has to be based on the assumption that whales keep growing. Can this assumption be proven scientifically?

Length and Weight

Few animals demonstrate extended growth, but all that do share similar characteristics in their bone structure. For an animal to keep growing in length, the vertebral column must also be able to continue growing. Animals that stop growing soon after sexual maturity, such as humans, have vertebral columns that cannot grow anymore. On either side of each vertebra there is a cap-like bone called the epiphysis. While the animal is growing, these "caps" are separated from the vertebra by a cartilaginous plate. For most mammals, after sexual maturity the caps fuse to the vertebra, and growing (in length) stops. For large whales, such as the rorquals, this fusion is delayed well past sexual maturity, and many older whales that have been caught have been found to have unfused epiphyses.

Given this evidence, it should not be surprising to find accounts of extremely large whales. For small whales, dolphins and porpoises, the epiphyses probably do fuse comparatively early, and the animals do have maximum lengths. In most cases, the measurements in this book indicate both the maximum records for each species and the average size. This average is the most likely size of whale for each species that you may see while out whale watching. A truth about nature is that there are always exceptions. For example, the maximum length given in this book for the Humpback Whale is 19 metres. This figure represents a reasonable maximum for the species. However, one female Humpback captured in shallow waters near Bermuda measured

Humpback Whale

a staggering 27 metres long. Exceptional whales do exist, and they remind us that our measurements and descriptions are guides, not rules.

The weights of the large rorqual, Bowhead and right whales are all subject to revision as we discover greater or more exceptional examples. Their weights are difficult to determine, but we can reasonably assume that the larger a whale specimen is, the more it weighs. The maximum weights recorded in this book are from unusually large whales. The generally accepted average weight is also included, and this figure corresponds to the average length.

Diving Depth

Other whale extremes are also well documented, such as the depth to which Sperm Whales can dive. Good science is about taking new information and shifting our framework to encompass it, rather than discounting evidence as mere calculation error or myth.

Sperm Whales were once thought to dive to a maximum depth of about 1500 metres. We now accept that Sperm Whales can dive much deeper. One of the deepest records is of two male

Sperm Whales that were killed upon surfacing from water that was more than 3000 metres deep. Both of them had freshly eaten, bottom-dwelling sharks in their stomachs, indicating that Sperm Whales can dive as deep as the sharks lived. Perhaps there is no maximum; the Sperm Whale is perfectly adapted to handle the stress of deep diving, and the determining factor of the dive depth may be availability of food or time without oxygen.

Longevity

Current research on Bowhead Whales has turned up startling evidence that these Arctic-dwelling whales may live for more than 200 years. Interest in Bowheads sparked when Inupiat hunters found old spear points and arrowheads buried deep in the flesh of a few individuals. Some of these stone points are dated at up to 200 years old, indicating the whale could be several years older than that. The traditional methods used by researchers to determine the age of a whale do not work on Bowhead Whales. A new method that studies the delicate layering in the lens of the eye is being employed to determine Bowhead ages. This method has shown several individuals at

Sperm Whale

Bowhead Whale

150 years
or more, and at least
one at 215 years old. We do not know the
maximum lifespan of a Bowhead Whale,
and some researchers suggest that 215
may be conservative. At more than 200
years old, Bowhead Whales are now considered to be some of the longest-lived
creatures on Earth, together with giant
tortoises (150 years old, with disputed
records at up to 200 years old) and giant
clams (up to 220 years old). The Blue
Whale is also considered a long-lived
species, but we have yet to determine the
age extremes for this species.

Whales vs. Dinosaurs

It is a popular belief that whales are
bigger than dinosaurs. Although whales
can be accurately measured for length,
weighing the largest of these beasts is
nearly impossible. As for dinosaurs, measuring their length involves speculation
and educated guessing. Many dinosaur
species are known only from a few separate bones, and determining the length of
a complete animal is sheer inference. To
complicate matters, paleontologists keep
turning up larger and larger specimens.
No one even knows which species is the
biggest dinosaur. Weighing a dinosaur is,

of course, impossible, and any given measurement is only theory.

Certain rules in biology make this
guessing game easier. We know, for example, that a marine animal can generally
have a greater body mass than a land animal because the water helps support its
weight. The conclusion is that Blue
Whales—at up to 181,400 kilograms—
win as the heaviest creatures, whereas
certain dinosaurs are the longest creatures
that ever lived. The longest dinosaurs
known include the Supersaurus, at 30–
40 metres, and both the Seismosaurus and
the recently discovered Argentinosaurus,
at 34–49 metres.

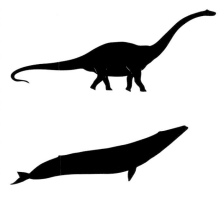

Intelligence and Whale Research

A common question people ask is, "How intelligent are whales?" The honest answer is that we do not know. Many studies have been done with whales to determine their intellectual abilities, but we do not have accurate ways of measuring intelligence in animals other than humans. Also, whales, dolphins and porpoises differ in intelligence amongst themselves. For example, most people accept that Orcas and Bottlenose Dolphins are more intelligent than river dolphins. Even how we define intelligence is ambiguous: it can mean independent thinking, analytical skills, understanding and evaluation skills or the ability to use reason and judgment in daily life. Intelligence can also be measured as a correlation between brain size and brain complexity.

Another difficulty arises in how we test cetacean intelligence. We require whales and dolphins to learn our signals and sounds, and then complete performance and ability tests.

The inherent flaw in these procedures is that we are not measuring how intelligent a whale is with such tests, we are only learning how well it does on tests designed by us. By learning the sounds, signals and performance abilities of whales and dolphins in their own environment, we may learn far more about the intelligence of these creatures.

Looking at the brain of a cetacean can give us an indication of its potential intelligence. Unfortunately, the ratio of body size to brain size (also called the "encephalization quotient") does not directly correlate with intelligence level. In absolute terms, Bottlenose Dolphins have larger brains than do humans, but their encephalization quotient is smaller. Bottlenose Dolphins and chimpanzees have a similar encephalization quotient. The complexity of a Bottlenose Dolphin's brain is higher, however, and it has a well-developed cerebral cortex. (The cerebral cortex is known to control the coordination of voluntary movement with

Bottlenose Dolphin

the senses, but it also contains centres responsible for memory, abstract thought, language and intellect.) Some people argue that this level of complexity serves to coordinate this dolphin's motor processes and echolocation, rather than being a sign of true intelligence. However, both odontocetes and mysticetes show a high level of complexity (relative to other mammals), and because mysticetes are not known to use echolocation, there is no clear evidence to support that argument.

Problem solving and the ability to learn are two well-accepted ways to assess intelligence. Whales in the wild show signs of teaching each other new things they have learned, and certainly mothers teach their calves many techniques for living. In captivity, cetaceans learn complex routines very quickly, and they even learn our language symbols. Studies with Bottlenose Dolphins indicate that they understand some abstract concepts like "sameness" and "difference." Using sign language, a dolphin easily understands the difference between "take the ball to the hoop" and "take the hoop to the ball." Dolphins seem quite capable of learning the basics of our language and signals, but we still have a long way to go to learn their sounds and language. Researchers still debate about definitions of language, and whether or not cetaceans have true language. Nevertheless, it is clear to any observer that dolphins use sounds between one another, and these sounds appear to have intention and even meaning.

Some dolphins and whales appear to have good levels of problem-solving ability, and there are several well-known examples of problem solving in wild cetaceans. In the wild, Bottlenose Dolphins have been observed using tools in problem situations, such as wielding the spines from a dead poisonous fish to oust an eel from its crevice. Many researchers believe that the cooperative bubble-netting demonstrated by Humpback Whales is an intentional act of cooperation to solve a common problem, although other researchers think this behaviour may be simply instinctive. During the heavy whaling years two centuries ago, Sperm Whales were frequently reported to swim and dive in directions upwind when pursued by a sailing vessel. Because sailing vessels cannot travel directly upwind, this behaviour could indicate a high level of reasoning or problem-solving ability in Sperm Whales, as well as an awareness of the consequences of being caught.

Problem-solving and behavioural studies are excellent forms of research that continually lead to a greater understanding of cetacean ability. The difficulty with problem-solving studies is in differentiating between instinctual responses and actual judgment and evaluation.

In Canada and neighbouring regions, whale research in the wild is becoming much more sophisticated. Satellite transmitters are being attached to many individuals to better understand their species' migration patterns. Photographic catalogues are used to identify hundreds of individual whales of many different species, especially Orca, Humpback and Blue whales. Orcas are reliably identified by the shape and scarring of their dorsal fin and by the shape and colouration of the "saddle" patch directly behind the dorsal fin. Humpback Whales can be recognized by the undersides of their tail flukes. The fluke colouration, shape and scarring patterns are used to identify individuals just as fingerprints are used to identify humans. Blue Whales are identified by their dorsal fin and the distinct mottled colouration on their sides and back. Knowing the individual whales means we can follow their movements and record their behaviours.

New diving technology allows divers to breathe underwater without releasing bubbles. Because many whales release bubbles as a threat or when they are alarmed, a diver who releases bubbles likely disturbs the whale and therefore alters its behaviour. Since researchers have been using these kind of diving units, called rebreathers, they have been able to observe male Humpbacks as they "sing." With standard scuba gear, the bubbles alerted the whale and it would immediately stop singing. The challenges of studying whales in the wild are great, but as we develop and apply new technology, we are able to learn more about the whales and their environment.

Male and female Orca dorsal fins

Whale Lore: from Legends to Modern Mythology

For many cultures, whales have been powerful symbols of creation, perfection and even prophecy. Perhaps the earliest known depiction of a cetacean is found in Norway, where an ancient carving of an Orca lingers on the coastal rocks; it is believed to be about 9000 years old. The ancient Greeks recognized the intelligence and friendliness of dolphins, and they regularly used dolphin motifs in their sculptures, frescoes, pottery, coins and paintings. Certain accounts of Greek mythology attach great meaning and spirituality to the dolphin. In one version of creation, all of life originated within a dolphin; hence the Greek species name *delphys*, which means "womb."

Historically, many indigenous coastal peoples included cetaceans in their mythology in some way. Whales, especially North Atlantic Right, Orca, Bowhead and Humpback whales, are an important part of native tradition—they are meshed into the social, religious and imaginative life of the people. In fact, because of the mythological importance of the Orca, it was never actively hunted by First Nations anywhere in Canada. The Inuit and Mi'kmaq also feared the Orca because these curious whales could so easily capsize their small canoes.

The Mi'kmaq and Abenaki people lived in the region of Atlantic Canada and New England long before the arrival of Acadian and British settlers. Their legends tell many stories of Glooscap, a mythical culture hero. One of the many tales about Glooscap explains the great tides in the Bay of Fundy. The legend says that the great Glooscap wanted to take a bath, and so he asked Beaver to build a dam across the mouth of the bay to trap the water. Pleased, Glooscap began his bath. Unfortunately, Whale was angered that the water had stopped flowing to her domain, and she came to the dam and poked her head over it to question Glooscap. Glooscap did not wish to anger Whale, so he got up and went back to land and instructed Beaver to take down the dam. Whale could not wait for Beaver to take the dam down, so with a stroke of her

On the West Coast, indigenous peoples so revered Orcas that the whales are commonly depicted on totem poles.

mighty tail she broke the dam and the water came rushing out. To this day the water still rushes in and out of the Bay of Fundy.

Although First Nations respected whales, many species were prized for their meat and oil. Indigenous peoples believed that whales, dolphins and porpoises lived in underwater villages similar to those of humans. On occasion, the chief whale would order an individual to allow itself to be caught by humans, to give food to the people in need. In gratitude, these people would throw the bones and intestines back into the water, in the belief that these remains would sink back to the whale's village and be renewed into another life.

In recent centuries, many humans feared whales, and contact with them was limited either to hunting or to occasional events of strandings. Mariners told outlandish stories of attacks by great sea creatures that spouted a toxic substance capable of peeling away your skin and blinding your eyes. Artists engraved terrible scenes of freakish giants capsizing boats and lashing out with their tails. Such perceptions were later replaced by phrases like "gentle giants" and stories of whales and dolphins saving human lives. These stories may be true, but the value and appreciation of cetaceans is not dependent solely on their interaction with humans. Indeed, the truth about whales lies somewhere in between the two extremes: they are not quite the gentle and obsequious giants that many people believe them to be, but they are certainly not evil behemoths that lurk beneath our boats, ready to strike.

Whale mythology is not limited to the historical perceptions and accounts of these great creatures. Throughout modern literature and art, whales have been exemplified, celebrated and somewhat idealized. Some famous works include Herman Melville's *Moby Dick*, Hollywood's *Star Trek: The Voyage Home* and *Free Willy*, television's *Flipper* and even Disney's *Pinocchio*. Such stories and films continually add to the rich tradition of whale lore.

Today, the perception and treatment of whales varies considerably among the different people of the world. Many people view whales as a superb opportunity to study mammalian adaptation, whereas others see whales as a source of entertainment. Many societies hunt whales for meat and profit; others consider whales to be creatures of inherent value outside of human valuation schemes.

Regardless of how we look at whales, we share an increasingly intricate relationship with them. Whales, dolphins and porpoises now attract millions of people each year to coastal areas throughout the world. Their special intrigue is a result of their intelligence and sheer magnificence. Watching a Humpback Whale breach and fall back into the water with a tremendous splash or seeing a dolphin's eye turn to look at you as it bowrides along your boat are extraordinary encounters that leave behind a feeling of contact with very special creatures. Cetaceans demand our respect as powerful creatures that can be friendly and inquisitive in most circumstances, but rightfully protective and aggressive when they are harassed.

Whales in Peril

Understanding Whaling

For centuries, whaling was considered a heroic profession that provided many necessary raw materials for a growing society. Whale parts were made into a staggering array of goods, making a list so long and composing so many unexpected products that it is no wonder the whaling industry was lucrative.

Whale oil was used in lamps, candles, lipsticks, lotions, soaps, shampoos, cooking goods, ice cream, crayons, glycerin (for explosives), machinery lubricants, leather processing, varnishes, adhesives—the list includes virtually everything that requires oil in some way. Baleen from whales has been used for only slightly fewer things, including, but not limited to, umbrella ribs, corsets, dress hoops, whips, window shutters, fishing rods, hairbrushes

and shoehorns. Whale meat and blubber was—and still is—eaten by many people; teeth were used as ivory for artworks or piano keys; bones were used for building structures or were ground down to make fertilizer; tendons were used for string and in place of catgut; whale skin was tanned to make leather, and the intestinal linings were stretched and used as transparent window panes. Even ambergris, a hard and waxy digestive by-product that forms in the gut of a Sperm Whale, was used as a fixative for perfumes and was once valued at over $800 per pound.

Most people who hunted whales made a tremendous effort to use every part of the whale and leave nothing to waste. The major difference in usage between groups of people was that some cultures were subsistence whalers and required whales for their survival, whereas other cultures were commercial whalers and used whales for

Explosive harpoon

profit. Even now, people in certain countries still hunt whales for sustenance, and others still hunt whales for profit.

The evidence of a successful whaling industry is indisputable. Over the last two centuries, millions of whales have been killed—so many, in fact, that several species may never recover. In the 1940s, when whale populations were at their lowest, no one could deny that if whaling was not dramatically curtailed, there would be no more large whales. From sheer necessity, the International Whaling Commission (IWC) formed in 1948 and began the first management strategy for the industry and the countries involved in whaling. Unfortunately, the quotas and agreements developed by the IWC were never adhered to, and whaling continued. Moreover, even if countries reported their annual whale takes to the IWC, most figures were as low as five percent of the actual number of whales that they killed.

A strong argument can be made that the small reduction in whaling that occurred up until the early 1990s happened not because of a global effort to save the whales, but because of a combination of two circumstances: primarily, that the whale populations were decimated, and catches of hundreds of whales each month were no longer possible; secondarily, that owing to the evolution of society, the demand for whale products decreased. Electricity greatly reduced the need for whale oil as a lighting agent, and plastic replaced baleen in many of its uses (and corsets, thankfully, went out of fashion).

In view of the large number of uses for whale products, and though it may not be condonable, it is at the very least understandable that the industry heightened to the point of over-exploiting the resource. After 1925, the combined effect of explosive harpoons, high-speed whaling vessels and floating whale-processing factories marked the peak of commercial whaling. The catch sizes over the next few decades alone were staggering, especially in Antarctic waters. The Fin Whale, previously too fast for the whaling vessels to catch, took the brunt of the onslaught, and nearly 750,000 were killed. Other large whales were taken as well: more than 360,000 Blue Whales, 200,000 Humpback Whales, 200,000 Sei Whales, nearly 400,000 Sperm Whales and more than 100,000 Minke Whales. These numbers represent just a short period in whaling history when whaling vessels could finally catch the faster whales. In the 1800s, the numbers were equally high for the slower whales, such as the right whales and the Bowhead Whale.

Only in the past 20 years has there been a real and obvious reduction in the number of whales killed annually, and the reduction is attributable to the efforts of conservation groups and a worldwide awareness of the plight of whales. Unfortunately, many species are far from safe, and their numbers are far from stable. The North Pacific Right Whale is undeniably the most endangered large whale—only a few hundred survive, and most biologists fear it is too late for this species.

Whaling in Atlantic Canada

The history of whaling in Atlantic Canada is long and certainly diverse and is largely composed of other countries whaling in these waters. The earliest whales hunted were Grey Whales and Humpback Whales. Putting a date on the first whaling event is nearly impossible because people were known to eat small whales as early as 6000 years ago. Whether these whales were found stranded or were actually hunted is unknown. Almost certainly, indigenous people hunted whales as early as 2000 years ago.

The Grey Whale once inhabited the waters of the east coast, but it disappeared from these waters by the early 1700s. Although the cause of its extirpation is not known for sure, it is likely that whaling is at least partly responsible. Grey Whales inhabit shallow coastal waters, making them easy targets for whalers.

As early as the mid-16th century, Basque whalers were regularly hunting right whales in Atlantic Canada. When lucrative whaling businesses developed in New England in the mid-18th century, whaling vessels regularly departed from Nantucket and New Bedford, some of which were destined for waters around Nova Scotia and Newfoundland. Sperm Whales were targeted because the spermaceti oil made smokeless and odourless candles. After 1850, whaling started to decline as kerosene, a superior fuel, became available.

Shore-based whaling developed in Newfoundland only in the early 20th century as a means of diversifying the local economy that was largely dependent on the cod fisheries. Shore-based whaling stations relocated sporadically as whale populations declined, and the entire industry met only limited success in a few localities. The second blow to whaling in Canada came from the development of plastics, which crippled the market for baleen. During the mid-1900s, plastics became easy to produce and readily available. By 1972, the Canadian government put an end to whaling.

Today, a few countries are still actively whaling, and some do so illegally. Fortunately, the numbers of whales taken annually are nowhere near historic records, but many cetacean species cannot tolerate more losses. Additionally, some First Nations are allowed to hunt limited numbers of whales, where subsistence whaling is both culturally important and

Grey Whale

35

necessary for survival. Inuit, for example, are permitted to hunt a predetermined number of Bowhead Whales in the Arctic.

Environmental Concerns

To simply criticize whaling as ecologically unsound is to impose a modern awareness on an industry whose products were historically in great demand. The industry supported and initiated many advancements in society and technology, and even the expansion of the Industrial Revolution was facilitated by whale-oil lubricants. Ironically, the whaling industry of North America made extensive contributions to whale science, and it is this core of knowledge about whales that now helps us protect and understand them. We have made many efforts to save the great whales from further decline as a result of whaling, but other, more subtle, threats exist that may be as dangerous to whales as the harpoon.

A sad fact is that the oceans, which cover 70 percent of the planet, are being used as dumping grounds for a plethora of wastes and by-products produced by modern civilization. Far too many countries have intentionally and accidentally dumped harmful wastes into the oceans, believing that the water will somehow hide or deal with the garbage that no one else will accept. But the oceans are not capable of sanitizing or hiding the billions of tons of toxic waste, agricultural chemicals, crude oil and plastic debris that are carelessly dumped into them, and these harmful substances are now affecting water quality and marine wildlife health around the world.

The magnitude of the problem is difficult to grasp. Many countries dump billions of tons of untreated wastewater into the oceans. There are approximately 65,000 chemicals that are commonly used in industry worldwide, and all of them end up in the oceans in some form or another. Chemical wastes—including DDT, organochlorides and heavy metals—stay in the environment for a long time. High concentrations can cause the death of sea animals immediately, whereas low concentrations can accumulate in their tissues and cause illness, disease and, ultimately, death. Whales that eat small fish or plankton with toxic or chemical waste in their bodies end up storing these harmful substances in their blubber. In the worst cases, dolphins that have died from chemical poisoning and washed up on shore are so laden with pollutants that they themselves are classified as toxic waste. Also, a female's milk, which is made from the body's fat reserves, can be so full of organochlorides and other contaminants that the nursing calf dies. This kind of poisoning of the ocean and marine creatures is extremely insidious and difficult to remedy. It is essential to the health of the oceans that people are educated about how harmful wastes can be, and about how to prevent the discharge from occurring.

One kind of pollution for which every person is responsible is plastic bags. Discarded plastic bags float in the water column and so closely resemble jellyfish and squid that many whales gulp them down. Eventually, a whale's digestive system becomes so blocked by plastic bags that it dies of starvation. Originally, when creatures that eat jellyfish or squid—such as sea turtles and whales—were found dead on shore, the cause of their deaths was unknown. It was only after autopsies that plastic bags were found to be the problem. Millions, or maybe even billions, of plastic bags are discarded every day, many of which will end up floating in the oceans.

There is no easy answer to the problem of marine pollution. Of course, the careless discarding of harmful products into the water must be curtailed, but the existing pollution in the water is not so easily cleaned up.

Fishing nets are also responsible for the deaths of innumerable cetaceans each year. The gill nets commonly used for fishing often catch small whales, dolphins and porpoises. Once caught in a net underwater,

a cetacean drowns because it must breathe air. When the nets are pulled in, the bodies of the drowned cetaceans must be untangled from the net. Eventually, a net is so full of holes that it is irreparable, and it is often discarded into the water. A discarded "ghost net" continues to catch sea creatures and small cetaceans while it floats freely through the ocean until it sinks to the bottom because of the weight of the bodies trapped in its mesh. Large whales may become entangled in ghost nets too, and they end up towing the net with them wherever they go. The net eventually digs into the whale's flesh, causing life-threatening injuries and preventing it from feeding properly.

If you are out whale watching and you see a whale entangled in a fishing net, the best course of action is to report this whale and its location to an emergency hotline. The telephone numbers of people who will help a whale in trouble are available on page 155 of this book.

Dolphin caught in fishing net

Whale Watching

Whale watching has become a world-wide activity that attracts millions of people each year. The coast of Atlantic Canada has many famous sites where whale watchers can easily see North Atlantic Right, Humpback, Fin and Northern Minke whales. Other species that can be seen unexpectedly at any time include Orcas and Blue, Sei and Sperm whales. Atlantic White-sided and White-beaked dolphins are regularly seen in certain locations. The preceding species are the most frequently seen cetaceans, but remember that every species in this book has been found in the waters of Atlantic Canada. Keep your eyes open for the rarer whales—positive sightings are worth reporting to local research stations.

The waters of Atlantic Canada, from the northern point of Labrador to the Bay of Fundy, comprise a unique diversity of marine mammals. The east coast of Canada has some of the most exciting places in the world for viewing and studying whales. Despite past whaling and current heavy boat traffic, the natural harbours and food-rich waters of the

coast form prime habitat for many species of whales. North Atlantic Right Whales perform their long migration along this coast, and some of the best-known and most-studied populations of Fin, Blue and Humpback whales also inhabit these waters. Humpback and North Atlantic Right whales feed in these waters, and as near-shore species they can even be viewed from land. The best time to see most whales is from June to September.

Although you may encounter whales throughout the coastal regions of Atlantic Canada, some places are better than others to find whales. The map on the facing page illustrates the best sites for whale watching, which also correlate to good availability of whale watching tours. With respect, the places where whales are sensitive to disturbance or places that are ecologically fragile have not been included. Nevertheless, some of the best whale watching sites in the world are here, ready for you to explore.

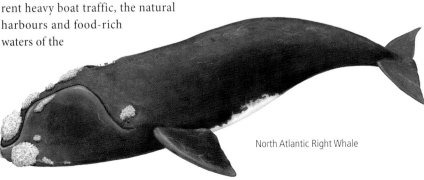

North Atlantic Right Whale

Top Whale Watching Sites

1	Rigolet	**7**	Lunenburg
2	Battle Harbour	**8**	Saint John
3	Bonavista	**9**	St. Andrews
4	St. John's	**10**	Grand Manan
5	Ingonish	**11**	Tiverton
6	Pleasant Bay/Cheticamp	**12**	Digby

Sea floor topography, especially around Nova Scotia and Newfoundland, plays an important role in whale abundance and diversity. Although we visualize the coast as the edge of the land, the continental shelf actually continues several hundred kilometres out to sea. The shelf regions of Atlantic Canada include the Labrador Shelf, Newfoundland Shelf, Grand Banks, Scotian Shelf and Bay of Fundy. Water depth over these shelf areas ranges from a mere 25 metres to just over 200 metres, though the average depth is about 90 metres. The Grand Banks is the widest shelf, extending as far as 480 kilometres from shore. Between the Grand Banks and the Scotian Shelf is the Laurentian Channel. This submerged valley is of glacial origin and is about 1400 kilometres long. Its depth varies between 180 and 550 metres, and its width ranges from 10 to 55 kilometres. Considerably deeper than the surrounding shelf waters, the Laurentian Channel provides habitat for many deepwater species of marine mammals, such as sperm and beaked whales. One of the most interesting features of the continental shelf is an area known as the Gully, near Sable Island on the edge of the Scotian Shelf. The Gully is the largest submarine canyon in eastern North America, and it reaches depths of almost 1500 metres. Officially a Marine Protected Area, the Gully has a rich diversity of marine life, including 21 species of deepsea corals, Sperm Whales and more than 200 non-migrating North Atlantic Bottlenose Whales.

Another factor that strongly influences marine life is the Gulf Stream. The Gulf Stream is a warm ocean current that originates off the tip of Florida and moves northward along the coast toward Canada. "Stream" is a misnomer, however, as the current is extremely powerful, and its volume is far greater than all the rivers emptying into the Atlantic. It is one of the strongest ocean currents in the world, second only to the Antarctic Circumpolar Current. In Atlantic Canada, the Gulf Stream meets and mixes with the cold Labrador Current over the Grand Banks. These mixing waters lift nutrients up from the bottom, thereby influencing the marine life of the region. Fish in the Grand Banks are among the most abundant in the world. Consequently, numerous species of whales and dolphins that prey on these fish are also abundant.

The northern coast of Labrador is subarctic and has a completely different array of marine wildlife. Bowhead Whales, Belugas and Narwhals can be found here, as well as countless seals and even Walruses.

There are many choices to make if you are to have a successful whale watching adventure. The time of year is important: catching the peak of migration makes for the best chances of seeing certain species. Humpback, Fin and North Atlantic Right whales are famous seasonal visitors in southern parts of this region. Other species, such as dolphins, Orcas and Northern Minke, Sperm and Long-finned Pilot whales, can be seen year-round. If you want to take a boat tour, you can choose between a day trip or a multiple-day cruise. Costs vary depending on how long of a trip you are taking.

Always take the time to learn about the person operating the tour. A tour leader should be knowledgeable about whale biology and be up to date on current locations of different whales. It is essential that the tour operator is responsible and behaves ethically around whales. Like people, whales have personalities and personal space requirements, and boaters who harass them (even unknowingly) can be extremely disruptive to the animal and can cause unnecessary stress and harm. In the worst cases, a whale that is badly harassed may show aggression toward boaters and can suffer stress or injuries. In the best cases, a whale may be comfortable with your presence and approach your boat on its own accord to get a better look at you. If you are the skipper of your own boat, know the basic guidelines for approaching whales. Although the following guidelines may appear to be strict, they ensure the safety of the whales and the boaters:

- minimum approach distance is 90 metres

- approach and leave whales at "no-wake" speed from the side or behind (never from ahead), with no sudden changes in speed or direction

- if a whale approaches, put the engine in neutral and allow it to pass

- never follow whales or herd, drive or separate them, particularly mothers and calves

- have only one vessel at a time at the minimum approach distance

- maintain a time limit of 30 minutes per vessel at the minimum distance

- swimmers should not approach within 45 metres.

Marine Mammal Regulations (MMR) in Canada prohibit the harassing, capturing or killing (outside of special permits) of any marine mammal. Anyone caught breaking this law is subject to fines and/or imprisonment. Most tour operators are knowledgeable and responsible and show genuine concern for the welfare of whales. If you encounter people who are not following proper conduct around whales, please speak up. Let them know they are interfering with and possibly harming the whales. If everyone acts responsibly, the whales will probably stay in the vicinity for everyone to enjoy.

The industry of whale watching is more than just the intrinsic pleasure of seeing these great creatures. The top whale watching regions in Atlantic Canada bring in millions of dollars every year, and, economically speaking, whale watching is worth far more than whaling. To look at whale watching in these monetary terms is important if whale conservation is to be politically and economically acceptable. However, attaching dollar figures to whale watching is superficial at best. How can we put a dollar figure on awe-inspiring experiences in the wild? As every whale watcher knows, the true value is in the extraordinary and breathtaking encounter with a wild whale.

About this Book

No matter where you are learning about whales, whether aboard a whale watching boat on the ocean or in the comfort of your own home, keep this book handy for quick reference about whales and other marine mammals. All the species you might encounter off the coast of Atlantic Canada are illustrated and described within this book. As well, historical and biological information is presented to give you a better understanding about whales in general.

About 26 whale species occur in the waters of Atlantic Canada. Of these, seven are baleen whales (mysticetes) and 19 are toothed whales (odontocetes). The most famous and commonly seen cetaceans in this region are the North Atlantic Right Whale, Humpback Whale, Fin Whale, Northern Minke Whale, Long-finned Pilot Whale, Atlantic White-sided Dolphin and Harbour Porpoise, but less common cetaceans may be encountered at any time.

The whales of Atlantic Canada are presented here in a generally accepted sequence that places the more closely related whales near one another. The scientific names and the ordering of the groups (genera) and species follow the "Revised checklist of North American mammals north of Mexico, 2003" (Occasional Paper No. 229, Museum of Texas Tech University, by Jones, Hoffmann, Rice et al. 2003). The section describing the other marine mammals in the region is similarly ordered, but is placed after the section on whales. The common names used in this book are widely accepted and frequently used names. Owing to discrepancies in the common names of many species, however, some species may be found under different names in other texts. Wherever applicable, the alternate common names are included in each entry as well as in the index.

The quick reference guide on pages 4 to 6 illustrates all the species in the book. It may help you identify species and groups at a glance, and it leads you to the detailed description of each species. The blows and dive sequences for selected species are also illustrated together on pages 23 and 24. The glossary (pages 152 to 154) defines some of the specialized terms that are used in talking about whales, and it also includes labelled diagrams of the main cetacean bodyparts.

Each species account includes a "Status" entry that gives information on the current conservation status of the species. Descriptions such as "endangered," "threatened" and "vulnerable" are official designations made by either the Committee on the Status of Endangered Wildlife in Canada (COSEWIC) or the International Union for Conservation of Nature (IUCN) and are defined in the glossary. Other descriptions appearing in the book, such as "common," "stable" or "declining," are used in accordance with current local research.

Each species account also includes a range map. Dark blue water indicates the known range for that species. You may find the range maps helpful when trying to determine the identity of a whale in the wild.

It should be noted that the lifecycles of many whales are described in terms of the animal's size instead of its age. Because of our limited understanding of cetaceans, we are unable to estimate an individual's age for most species, whereas length can be readily measured in the field.

Sample range map

Because some whales are so very large, it can be hard to get a good visual idea of their size. To help you with this task, below the size measurements we show a scaled comparison between an average-sized individual of each species and either a human diver (about 1.8 metres tall) or a school bus (about 11 metres long).

Once you have learned to identify whales and you are familiar with their natural history, enjoy them! Whales are marvelous creatures, and watching them can be a thrilling and memorable experience.

These silhouettes will help give an idea of scale when considering the size of a whale.

The "Similar Species" section in each species account lists other whales or marine mammals that could easily be confused with the animal you are reading about. Be sure to check these other species before you decide on the identity of an animal in the wild.

Orca

Whale Tales & Record Breakers

This section attempts to clarify some of the frequently asked questions about whales and whale extremes. Keep in mind, however, that these answers are not absolute. As we learn and discover more about the marine world, we have to continually update our record sheets.

How many different whales are there in the world?
There are currently 88 known species of whales, dolphins and porpoises.

What is the largest whale in the world?
Blue Whale: maximum record 34 m long.

What is the smallest whale in the world?
Franciscana (river dolphin): 1.4–1.8 m long.

What is the heaviest whale in the world?
Blue Whale: maximum record 181,400 kg.

What is a Whale Shark?
A Whale Shark is a shark, not a whale. The modifier "whale" is used because this shark is very big (up to 18 m long).

What is the fastest whale in the world?
Atlantic White-sided Dolphin: 59 km/h.

What is the longest-lived whale?
Bowhead Whale: more than 200 years.

What is the deepest-diving whale?
Sperm Whale: deepest record 3050 m.

How long can a whale hold its breath?
Sperm Whale: confirmed record 2 hours, 18 minutes.

What is the longest migration made by a whale?
Grey Whale: round trip (one year) 20,000 km.

How much food can a whale eat in one day?
Blue Whale: up to 6500 kg.

What is the longest pregnancy for a whale?
Orca: 15 to 16 months.

What is the rarest whale in the world?
Yangtze River Dolphin (China): fewer than 100 remaining.

What is the loudest sound made by a whale?
Blue Whale: 188 decibels, measurable for at least 2400 km underwater.

Which whale has the most baleen plates?
Fin Whale: 360 plates (on average).

Which whale has the longest baleen?
Bowhead Whale: 4.3 m. One disputed report of 5.8 m.

Which whale has the most teeth?
Spinner Dolphin: 224.

Which whale has the longest teeth?
Narwhal: a single tusk can reach 3 m long. One in 500 males has two tusks.

Baleen Whales

Rorqual Family (Balaenopteridae)

The rorquals number only six species worldwide, and five of them may be seen off the coast of Atlantic Canada. They include some of the largest whales on earth—the Blue Whale is reputed to be one of the largest animals that has ever lived. The name "rorqual" is derived from the Norwegian word *rorhval*, meaning "furrow," which refers to the pleats, or folds, in the skin of the throat. These throat pleats expand during feeding, allowing the throat to distend to an enormous, balloon-like shape when the whale gulps a massive volume of food-rich water into its mouth. The whale does not swallow the water; instead, the pleats contract and the tongue moves forward to push the water out through the baleen. Any crustaceans or fish are trapped inside the mouth and swallowed whole. The only whales outside the rorqual family that have throat pleats are the Grey Whale and the beaked whales, but their pleats are relatively few and have greatly reduced efficacy.

Rorquals are easily identified by their pointed snout, flattened head, long and slender body and relatively small dorsal fin, which sits about two-thirds of the way down the back. When a rorqual's mouth is open, the short baleen, which is continuous around the front of the jaw, is visible.

Fin Whale

Right Whale Family (Balaenidae)

This family includes two kinds of whales: the right whales and the Bowhead Whale. The Bowhead Whale is found only in arctic and subarctic waters. Right whales have a much larger distribution.

The endangered right whales were once found throughout the world's cold and temperate oceans. Their total population now is probably only a few thousand individuals. There is much argument about whether there are one, two or three species of right whales. Many scientists believe there is only one species worldwide, *Eubalaena glacialis*, while others feel strongly that this name represents only the North Atlantic population and that the Southern Hemisphere has a different species (*E. australis*). The third species (*E. japonica*) inhabits the north Pacific from the Sea of Okhotsk to the Bering Sea.

Among the most distinct features of a right whale are the growths over its face and head. These callosities are masses of keratin topped with barnacles and teeming with whale lice. The whale lice may be pink, white, orange or yellow, and they give the callosities their unique colour. The origin of these callosities is intriguing—they grow in all the places on the whale's head where a human would have hair. Specifically, they are found on the "chin," the upper "lip" and above the eye. Keratin makes up both fingernails and hair in other mammals, and this fact may explain the origin of callosities in right whales.

North Atlantic Right Whale

Northern Minke Whale

Balaenoptera acutorostrata

The Northern Minke Whale, the smallest of the rorquals, is relatively common in Atlantic Canada. Despite their numbers, minke whales are elusive and difficult to spot because they spend less time at the surface than other whales—they usually take only five to seven breaths before they go under again. As well, minke whales rarely make a visible blow, and they usually travel singly—one little dorsal fin against an ocean of waves is easy to overlook. Yet there are cases where a minke whale has surfaced right next to a boat, much to the surprise of the people aboard. Such occurrences are fleeting; the whale rapidly takes a breath and disappears as quickly as it came.

Several researchers who have studied minke whales consider them extremely intelligent and adaptable. Minke whales are known to look for flocks of gulls, murres or auklets on the water—a flock of feeding birds advertises the whereabouts of a school of fish, making the fish an easy lunch for the whale. Although minke whales in equatorial and southern waters frequently use this tricky technique, the behaviour is not as common in northern areas.

The study of minke whales is still in its early stages, owing partly to their elusiveness, but also to their wide distribution. People wanting to study right whales, for example, know exactly where to find them, but minke whales can be anywhere, and we have yet to determine their behaviour patterns. It is known that many

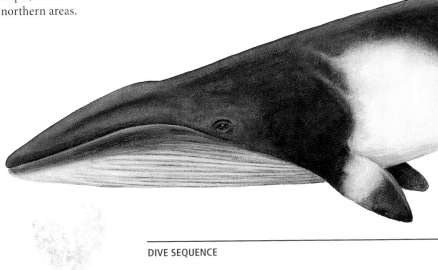

DIVE SEQUENCE

RANGE: widely distributed throughout the world: in summer, common in cold polar waters; in winter, migrates to more temperate waters.

OTHER NAMES: Common Minke Whale, Piked Whale, Sharp-headed Finner, Little Finner, Lesser Finback, Lesser Rorqual.

STATUS: insufficient data worldwide; locally common.

ADULT LENGTH: up to 11 m; average 8.2 m.

ADULT WEIGHT: up to 14,000 kg; average 9000 kg.

BIRTH LENGTH: 2.4–2.7 m.

BIRTH WEIGHT: 350 kg.

studied. New advances in satellite and radio taps, however, may help fill in some of the knowledge gaps.

In the 1980s, minke whales were the most heavily hunted baleen whales in the world. The populations of the larger whales had declined so dramatically by then that whalers from many countries started to take these small rorquals instead. Minkes are still more

minke whales migrate between warm and cold waters each year, but some are believed to stay in one region year-round. The Northern Minke Whale's winter mating and calving waters in the North Atlantic are not well

heavily hunted than almost any other baleen whale, but new regulations and international efforts have protected them in many parts of their range.

DESCRIPTION: The Northern Minke Whale is striking, with whorls of white over its dark back and white "epaulets" on its flippers. On some individuals, the entire flipper may be white; on others, the white may be just a narrow band or even nonexistent. This variation in flipper markings is regionally specific, and it might indicate different subspecies. The colouration over the back varies considerably throughout a minke's range: it can be dark slate grey, nearly black, deep bluish or dark brown. A minke whale's undersides are white or nearly white, and there are often swirls of white behind the flippers and again below the dorsal fin. This whale's overall appearance in the water is very sleek and streamlined. Its head is quite pointed, with a prominent splashguard before the blowhole and a distinct single ridge to the snout. Relative to most other rorquals, the Northern Minke Whale has a large, curved dorsal fin. Females are generally larger than males.

Flipper variations

BALEEN WHALES

areas of high food concentration, a hundred or more minke whales may occur together.

FEEDING: Like the larger rorquals, the Northern Minke Whale feeds mainly on krill, but it also eats some other invertebrates and small fish. It commonly lunge-feeds by swimming into a school of krill or small fish and gulping a large volume of food-filled water into its mouth. Its throat stretches like a big balloon, and as the whale closes its mouth and the throat pleats contract, the water is forced out through the baleen but the organisms in the water are trapped in the mouth, and the whale uses its tongue to wipe the creatures off the baleen so it can swallow them.

REPRODUCTION: Minkes probably mate in late winter, but no calving waters have been found for the North Atlantic population, and very little is known about their reproductive cycle. The gestation period is 10 months. The nursing period is short, 3 to 6 months. Healthy females will mate again within a few months of giving birth, resulting in 1 calf every 12 to 14 months. Male minke whales are sexually mature when they reach about 7 m in length, and females when they are 7.3 m long.

BLOW: The Northern Minke Whale may make a small, quick, bushy blow that reaches a maximum height of about 2.7 m. The blow is rarely visible, especially on warm days. On a very calm day, you may hear the blow rather than see it.

OTHER DISPLAYS: When a minke whale breaches, it comes far enough out of the water to expose its dorsal fin. The whale leaves the water at about a 45 degree angle, and it usually does not twist or turn as it comes down with a tremendous splash. This whale often arches back into the water headfirst, so the breach looks more like a dive than a belly flop.

GROUP SIZE: Minke whales are seen either singly or in groups of 2 to 4 individuals. In

SIMILAR SPECIES: The Sei Whale (p. 52) is almost twice the size and lacks white "epaulets" on its flippers.

Sei Whale

Sei Whale

Balaenoptera borealis

DESCRIPTION: The Sei Whale resembles the larger Fin Whale (p. 58) and the similarly sized Bryde's Whale (*B. edeni*), and the three species can be hard to distinguish where they occur together. The Sei Whale is mainly dark grey, blackish or bluish grey, with pale grey or whitish undersides, and it may have irregular, pale scars and marks along its body. Its baleen is finer and silkier than that of other rorquals, and its throat pleats are fewer and shorter. The dorsal fin is slender, upright and curved on the trailing edge. The flippers are dark on both sides, and they have pointed tips. The tail flukes are small relative to the size of the body. Females are generally larger than males.

BLOW: The Sei Whale makes a blow that is similar to, but smaller than, those of the Blue Whale (p. 54) and the Fin Whale. The blow is generally narrow, but not dense, and it may be up to 3 m tall. It is sometimes mildly heart-shaped.

OTHER DISPLAYS: Sei Whales breach infrequently and rarely more than once at a time. They leave the water at a low angle and re-enter with a splash.

GROUP SIZE: Sei Whales are seen either singly or in groups of up to 5 individuals. Feeding waters attract larger numbers.

FEEDING: The Sei Whale feeds primarily on small schooling fish or invertebrates such as squid, krill and copepods. Its feeding style is similar to a right whale's: rather than lunge-feeding like the other rorquals, the Sei Whale tends to skim steadily through food-rich water.

DIVE SEQUENCE

RANGE: found in deep, temperate waters worldwide: in summer, may travel to food-rich subpolar waters; for the rest of the year, primarily found at lower latitudes.

OTHER NAMES: Pollack Whale, Coalfish Whale, Sardine Whale, Japan Finner, Boreal Rorqual, Rudolphi's Rorqual.

STATUS: endangered (IUCN).

ADULT LENGTH: up to 21 m; average 15 m.

ADULT WEIGHT: up to 32,000 kg; average 25,000 kg.

BIRTH LENGTH: 4.3–4.9 m.

BIRTH WEIGHT: about 730 kg.

SIMILAR SPECIES: The Northern Minke Whale (p. 48) is much smaller and usually has white "epaulets" on its flippers; the Fin Whale (p. 58) is larger, has a white lower right jaw and has more and longer throat pleats; the Blue Whale (p. 54) is much larger and has a relatively smaller dorsal fin.

REPRODUCTION: Sei Whales mate and bear their young in mid-winter. The gestation period is 11½ months. Each female bears a single calf. These whales are sexually mature when they are about 95 percent of their total adult length.

Fin Whale

Blue Whale

Balaenoptera musculus

Bigger than a dinosaur, bigger than a jet plane, bigger than three school buses—the words we use to describe the size of the Blue Whale hardly do justice to this leviathan. We cannot easily comprehend or describe how large the Blue Whale is, and perhaps this difficulty is reflected in the 18th-century humour used to scientifically name the species. As if in jest, because any word we could use to describe this whale would fall short of capturing its true immensity, the Latin word *musculus*, meaning "little mouse," was used. The Blue Whale is so manifestly not a mouse that we can only smile at the comparison.

The Blue Whale is the most famous record-breaker in the animal kingdom. Not only is it the largest creature alive, and one of the largest there ever has been, but it is also the loudest—its low-frequency pulses have been measured at up to 188 decibels, as loud as a space shuttle engine. At birth, a Blue Whale calf is 7 m long, which is already larger than at least two-thirds of whales at their full adult length, even though the gestation period—about a year—is pretty typical of baleen whales. The calf grows at an incredible rate: it puts on a staggering 90 kg a day, nursing 190 L of milk from its mother every day, and a weaned juvenile (about eight months old) is about 15 m long. As adults, the largest individuals may eat up to 3600 kg of food a day during summer. An adult's heart is as large as a compact car, and a small child could crawl through the arteries. A male's penis is about 3 m long.

Another record the Blue Whale holds, unfortunately, is that it is one of the most

DIVE SEQUENCE

RANGE: usually found in open waters; although distribution appears to be worldwide, it is not continuous.

OTHER NAMES: Sulphur-bottom, Sibbald's Rorqual, Great Northern Rorqual.

STATUS: endangered (IUCN).

ADULT LENGTH: up to 34 m; average 26 m.

ADULT WEIGHT: up to 181,000 kg; average 109,000 kg.

BIRTH LENGTH: about 7 m.

BIRTH WEIGHT: about 2300 kg.

... endangered large cetaceans in the world. At the height of the whaling industry in the late 1800s and early 1900s, Blue Whales were relentlessly pursued. By 1950, the species was declared endangered. In 1966, the International Whaling Commission gave a protected status to the Blue Whale, and it is slowly recovering. The total population is estimated to be about 10,000 individuals, but this number could be as high as 20,000.

Although there is no guarantee of seeing a Blue Whale, there are good chances to see one of these magnificent creatures in some regions. They are rare in shelf waters, but they are present for much of the year in the Gulf of St. Lawrence. Blues are strongly nomadic, and they do not stay in the same waters for more than 10 days. There is a moderate migration between northern (polar) waters in summer and southern (equatorial) waters in winter. Although some species of whales fast when they are in their warm winter waters, there is evidence that Blues feed year-round, likely a necessity considering their size.

DESCRIPTION: The enormous Blue Whale is typically deep slate blue or greyish in colour, with variable pale grey or white mottling over the back. Its undersides are lighter, ranging in colour from pale blue-grey to white to yellowish. A film of diatoms on the pale undersides results in yellowish bellies on some individuals and gives rise to the alternate name "Sulphur-bottom." The Blue Whale has a broad, flattened head, a large splashguard before the blowhole and a pale throat with 55 to 88 pleats. The relatively tiny dorsal fin is located about ¾ of the way down the body. The flippers are long, slender and darker above than below. The tail stock is very thick. The flukes are narrow and slightly notched, and the tail is very wide from tip to tip—almost ¼ of the body length in width. Females are generally larger than males.

BLOW: The blow of the Blue Whale is distinctive: the narrow column of spray can rise at least 11 m high, and it can be seen even at a distance of 5–8 km.

a period of up to 6 minutes, and then it will dive for 10 to 15 minutes.

GROUP SIZE: Blue Whales are typically seen singly or in pairs. Even when food-rich water attracts high densities, they remain as singles or pairs.

FEEDING: The Blue Whale specializes in eating krill—shrimp-like creatures that are less than 13 mm in length—and it rarely eats anything else. A Blue Whale usually rises up into a school of krill from below, gulping in hundreds of gallons of seawater. The water is squeezed out through the baleen either rapidly or over the course of several minutes.

REPRODUCTION: Gestation lasts 11 to 12 months, and the peak calving period appears to be during winter, when the whales are at low latitudes. Calves are weaned when they are about 8 months old. Both sexes reach sexual maturity when they are at least 80 percent of their adult length—about 10 years old.

SIMILAR SPECIES: The Fin Whale (p. 58) is smaller and has a larger dorsal fin; the Sei Whale (p. 52) is much smaller and has a larger dorsal fin.

OTHER DISPLAYS: Not surprisingly, the Blue Whale is not acrobatic, but a juvenile may breach and make a tremendous splash as it falls back into the water, on either its side or its belly. An adult's dive sequence is marked initially by the tall blow; then the whale's long back rolls over the surface. The dorsal fin appears well after the head has disappeared and the blow has dispersed. During its dive sequence, a Blue Whale may surface several times over

Fin Whale

Sei Whale

Fin Whale

Balaenoptera physalus

DESCRIPTION: The unusual Fin Whale has a striking asymmetry of colouration on its head: the right side of the outer lower "lip" and the baleen on the right side are whitish, whereas the counterparts on the left side are grey. Oddly enough, the mouth cavity and tongue are grey on the right and white on the left. There is a distinct pale grey, V-shaped mark behind the head. The overall body colour is dark grey, silvery grey or brownish black, and the undersides are white. The dorsal fin is small and slanted backward. The flippers and flukes are dark on top and white below. There is a distinct ridge on the back from the dorsal fin to the flukes. Females are generally larger than males.

BLOW: The Fin Whale's narrow blow is quite dense and is 4–6 m high, making it visible from far away.

OTHER DISPLAYS: Fin Whales may make spectacular breaches, leaving the water at 45 degrees, but they rarely show their dorsal fin. They may twist in the air as they come down with a thunderous splash.

GROUP SIZE: Fin Whales are occasionally found singly or in pairs, but more typically they are found in groups of 3 to 10 individuals.

FEEDING: The main diet of the Fin Whale includes schooling fish, krill, squid, copepods and other invertebrates. Lunge-feeding, during which the whale often turns on its right side, is commonly seen.

REPRODUCTION: Fin Whales mate in late winter. About 11 months later, 1 calf is born. Males are sexually mature at 90 percent of their adult length; females at 75 to 80 percent.

DIVE SEQUENCE

RANGE: found worldwide in temperate and subpolar waters.

OTHER NAMES: Common Rorqual, Finback, Razorback, Herring Whale, Finner.

STATUS: endangered (IUCN).

ADULT LENGTH: up to 27 m; average 21 m.

ADULT WEIGHT: up to 127,000 kg; average 73,000 kg.

BIRTH LENGTH: 6.1–6.7 m.

BIRTH WEIGHT: about 1800 kg.

SIMILAR SPECIES: The Blue Whale (p. 54) is larger and has a smaller dorsal fin; the Sei Whale (p. 52) is smaller, has fewer and shorter throat pleats and does not have a white lower right jaw.

Blue Whale

Sei Whale

Humpback Whale

Megaptera novaeangliae

Humpback Whales are renowned for both their extensive migrations and their haunting songs. They are commonly seen by whale watchers, and they seem to enjoy performing for their boat-bound admirers. Other than brief bouts of fighting between males during the winter breeding season, Humpback Whales have gentle and docile natures.

In summer, Humpbacks feed and socialize off Atlantic Canada. In winter, they migrate south to Caribbean waters, where they mate and calve. There are six major feeding aggregations of Humpback Whales in the North Atlantic. Three of these are the Gulf of Maine aggregation (including the Bay of Fundy), the Gulf of St. Lawrence aggregation and the Newfoundland/Labrador aggregation. These areas offer some of the best opportunities in the world to view feeding Humpback Whales. By September, the whales begin their migration south. In general, Humpbacks migrate as much as 8000 km between high latitude summer feeding waters and low latitude mating and calving waters. Although feeding and mating waters are distinct between different populations of Humpbacks,

DIVE SEQUENCE

RANGE: found worldwide, from polar to tropical waters; migrates seasonally, so some regions have higher densities than others.

STATUS: threatened (COSEWIC); locally common.

ADULT LENGTH: up to 19 m; average 14 m.

ADULT WEIGHT: up to 48,000 kg; average 27,000 kg.

BIRTH LENGTH: 4–4.9 m.

BIRTH WEIGHT: 900–1800 kg.

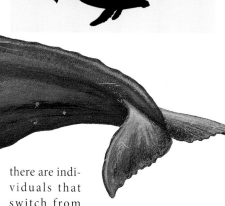

there are individuals that switch from one population to another.

The song of the Humpback Whale is one of the most impressive sounds in the animal kingdom. A Humpback can sing for a few minutes to half an hour, and an entire performance can go on for several days, with only short breaks between each song.

The songs are composed of trills, whines, snores, wheezes and sighs, and when sung in a repeating pattern, the result is mysterious and hauntingly beautiful. Although the true meaning of the Humpback's song eludes us, we do know that only the males sing and that they perform mainly during the breeding season. Many animals use sound to attract the opposite sex, which may be the primary function of the Humpback's songs.

Male Humpbacks become very aggressive toward one another and battle to determine dominance in their winter breeding waters. A dominant male becomes the escort to a female with a calf. Presumably, a female with a calf is one that is, or will soon be, receptive to mating.

DESCRIPTION: The Humpback Whale is slightly more robust in the body than are other rorquals. The overall body colour is either dark grey or dark slate blue, and the undersides may be the same colour as the back or nearly white. The slender head bears many knobs and projections around the snout, and the mouth line arches downward to the eye. There are 12 to 36 pleats on the pale throat. The flippers are long and knobby and have a varying pattern of white markings. The tail flukes are strongly swept back and have irregular trailing edges. Like the flippers, the flukes have unique white markings that can be used to identify individual whales. The dorsal fin can be small and stubby or high and curved, and several small knuckles are visible on the dorsal ridge between the fin and the tail. Humpbacks often host barnacles and whale lice. Females are generally larger than males.

Fluke variations

and show a strongly arched back. The tail flukes are lifted high only on deep dives.

GROUP SIZE: Humpbacks commonly live in small groups of 2 or 3 members, but some groups may have 15 members, and Humpbacks are occasionally seen singly. Good feeding and breeding waters usually draw large groups.

FEEDING: The Humpback Whale feeds mainly by lunge-feeding or by bubble-netting, but much individual variation occurs in feeding styles. Its major foods are krill and schooling fish, such as anchovies and sardines.

REPRODUCTION: The courtship behaviour of Humpbacks is elaborate and involves lengthy bouts of singing by the males. Mating usually occurs in warm waters, and single calves are born following a gestation period of about 11½ months. The calves stay close to their mothers and nurse for about 1 year. Females reach sexual maturity when they are about 12 m long, and males when they are at least 11.5 m long.

BLOW: The Humpback Whale makes a thick, orb-shaped blow that can reach up to 3 m high and is visible at a great distance. From directly in front or behind, the blow may appear slightly heart-shaped.

OTHER DISPLAYS: An acrobatic whale, the Humpback dazzles whale watchers with high breaches that finish in a tremendous splash. Other behaviours that it may repeat several times include lob-tailing, flipper-slapping and spy-hopping. Humpbacks are often inquisitive, and they may approach boats if the boaters are non-harassing. When Humpbacks breathe and dive, they roll forward through the water

SIMILAR SPECIES: The North Atlantic Right Whale (p. 64) has callosities instead of knobs on its head, and it has much shorter flippers.

North Atlantic Right Whale

North Atlantic Right Whale

Eubalaena glacialis

Over the past few decades, the right whales have been renamed and reclassified several times. Although some scientists still maintain there is only one species worldwide, there are currently three accepted species: the North Atlantic Right Whale, the North Pacific Right Whale (*E. japonica*) and the Southern Right Whale (*E. australis*). The highly endangered right whales were the most heavily pursued whales during the height of whaling. The name "right whale" is derived from mariners referring to it as the "right" whale to hunt: it is large, it has thick blubber and long baleen, and it swims slowly. The right whales were the first whales to be hunted commercially, and hundreds of thousands of them were killed to feed the demand for whale oil and other whale products. By 1920, the North Atlantic Right Whale was nearly extinct. Even today, there are fewer than 350 right whales in the North Atlantic. The North Pacific Right Whale is even worse off; there may not even be 100 of them remaining. In the Southern Hemisphere, the numbers are better—as many as 12,000 Southern Right Whales still exist.

The chances of seeing a North Atlantic Right Whale in certain areas of Atlantic Canada are excellent, especially in the Bay of Fundy, Roseway Basin off Nova Scotia and the Gulf of St. Lawrence.

DIVE SEQUENCE

BALEEN WHALES

RANGE: found in polar and temperate waters of the North Atlantic; favours offshore waters rather than open ocean.

OTHER NAMES: Northern Right Whale, Black Right Whale, Biscayan Right Whale.

STATUS: endangered (IUCN).

ADULT LENGTH: up to 18 m; average 14 m.

ADULT WEIGHT: up to 86,000 kg; average 54,000 kg.

BIRTH LENGTH: 4.6–6.1 m.

BIRTH WEIGHT: about 900 kg.

When North Atlantic Right Whales are seen in the wild, they can be quite approachable and inquisitive. Sometimes these whales are playful, bumping and pushing floating objects in the water. As a cautionary note, these qualities of inquisitiveness and playfulness can result in a whale playing near or with your boat. Some kayakers have been surprised when their boats were bumped or lifted in friendly jest.

As everyone knows, the greatest record-breaking animal in the world is the Blue Whale. The understated right whales, however, win a few titles of their own. Although it is not a very noble record to hold, right whales may well be the slowest whales on Earth. Less flattering still, these whales are one of the fattest whales, considering their weight per foot of body length. Their large tail is the broadest, relative to the length of the body. The one title these whales carry that may place them in the realm of nobility among cetaceans is for the largest testicles. With testes weighing in at 500 kg (each!), no other creature in the history of the world is as well-endowed. By comparison, the testes of the now-humbled Blue Whale weigh a mere 68 kg.

DESCRIPTION: The robust North Atlantic Right Whale is easy to distinguish because of the callosities on its head and its lack of a dorsal fin. Distinct callosities grow on the "chin," on the rostrum, in front of the blowhole and above the eye. The body is nearly black, dark blue or dark brown, and it may show slight mottling or even patchy white spots on the belly. The mouth line is strongly arched upward and then drops nearly vertically to meet the eye. There is a distinct indentation behind the blowhole and then a bulge continuing over the back. The baleen plates can be as long as 2.4 m. The flippers are large and spatula-shaped, and they are dark on both sides. At close range, the finger bones in a flipper can be seen as distinct ridges. The flukes, also dark both above and below, are smooth and pointed and have a noticeable notch in the middle. Females are generally larger than males.

BLOW: When viewed from the front or the rear, a right whale's distinctive blow is widely V-shaped. The sound is loud, and the spray can reach a height of 5 m.

Callosities (front view)

shape of the baleen makes the mouth look like a cave. As the whale progresses through a concentration of copepods, the water enters the "cave" and passes through the baleen. All of the creatures are trapped against the silky hairs of the baleen plates and eventually swallowed. This whale skim-feeds wherever the food is present—at the surface or at depth.

REPRODUCTION: The right whales have never managed to recover their numbers the way other whales have. The reasons are not clear, but the combination of isolated populations and a slow reproductive rate may be responsible. Females give birth only once every 3 or 4 years. Although these whales court and mate year-round, peak conception appears to be in winter, as is calving, which indicates a gestation period of about 1 year. Both sexes are sexually mature when they are 75 to 80 percent of the adult length.

OTHER DISPLAYS: The North Atlantic Right Whale is quite acrobatic, considering its bulk. It often breaches, lob-tails, flipper-slaps and spy-hops. When it lob-tails, it may invert in the water to such a great extent that it appears to be doing a headstand.

GROUP SIZE: These right whales are typically found in small groups of 2 or 3 individuals. Sometimes a group numbering up to 12 members is seen. Seasonal feeding waters attract larger numbers of whales at certain times.

FEEDING: A remarkably efficient filter-feeder, the North Atlantic Right Whale feeds on some of the smallest zooplankton in the sea. The primary food is tiny krill and other copepods. To feed, the whale swims slowly with its mouth open. The unique

SIMILAR SPECIES: The Humpback Whale (p. 60) has knobs instead of callosities on its head and has much longer flippers; the Bowhead Whale (p. 68) lacks callosities entirely.

Humpback Whale

Bowhead Whale

Bowhead Whale

Balaena mysticetus

DESCRIPTION: The Bowhead Whale is a large, rotund whale with a strongly bowed mouth line. It is mainly black in colour, though it may have a white "chin" with a series of black spots running through it. The body is generally smooth, free of both barnacles and callosities. The upper jaw is very narrow when viewed from above, and there is a prominent indentation behind the blowhole. There is no dorsal fin. The flippers are dark on both sides. There may be a pale grey ring around the tail stock. The flukes, which are up to 7 m wide, are also dark on both sides. The Bowhead's baleen is longer than that of any other whale—it is usually 3–4 m long, with a maximum recorded length of 5.2 m—and there is no baleen at the front of the mouth. Females are generally larger than males.

BLOW: This whale has widely separated blowholes. The resulting blow is broadly V-shaped, and it can rise up to 7 m.

OTHER DISPLAYS: Before a dive, a Bowhead Whale may raise its tremendous flukes into the air. This whale also breaches occasionally, with ½ to ¾ of its body leaving the water vertically and falling on its side with a tremendous splash.

GROUP SIZE: Bowheads are seen either singly or in small groups of up to 6 members. Good feeding sites may attract up to 15 whales. Rarely,

DIVE SEQUENCE

RANGE: found primarily in western arctic seas (whaling decimated much of its eastern arctic populations); has a short, nomadic migration that matches the advance and retreat of the sea ice.

OTHER NAMES: Greenland Right Whale.

STATUS: endangered (COSEWIC).

ADULT LENGTH: up to 20 m; average 17 m.

ADULT WEIGHT: up to 109,000 kg; average 73,000 kg.

BIRTH LENGTH: 3.7–4.6 m.

BIRTH WEIGHT: about 900 kg.

REPRODUCTION: As the ice retreats in summer, these whales move northward to high arctic water, where they mate. Gestation is 13 months, and a female gives birth to 1 calf in August, alternating at least 2 years between pregnancies. Calves nurse for about 1 year, and both sexes become sexually mature at about 12 m in length. Bowhead Whales are believed to live for over 200 years.

SIMILAR SPECIES: The North Atlantic Right Whale (p. 64) has callosities on its head, especially over the eye and rostrum.

North Atlantic Right Whale

during migration events, Bowheads may form loose groups of up to 60 individuals.

FEEDING: Bowhead Whales are often seen skim-feeding through waters rich in krill and other copepods. Several whales may form a U-shaped group while skim-feeding in the same direction at the same speed.

Toothed Whales

Beluga and Narwhal Family (Monodontidae)

This small family of whales includes only the Beluga and the Narwhal, polar species that follow the seasonal formation and retreat of ice in the Arctic. These two whales are known to intermingle, and temporary nursery colonies have even formed with members from both species. Belugas are more widespread than Narwhals, and in Atlantic Canada they can be found on the northern coast of Labrador. A remnant population is also found in the St. Lawrence River area. Belugas and Narwhals do not have fused neck vertebrae—an unusual characteristic for cetaceans—and they are able to turn their heads, nod and look around in a manner unlike other whales.

Ocean Dolphin Family (Delphinidae)

This large family of toothed whales represents the true ocean dolphins, and it includes some of the most well-known cetaceans—aquariums, movies and anecdotal accounts have made Bottlenose Dolphins and Orcas world-famous cetaceans. There are at least 38 delphinid species worldwide, but some evidence indicates that certain species, like the Bottlenose Dolphin, may actually be two or three distinct species. At least eight species of delphinids exist in the waters of Atlantic Canada.

Although many people call the Orca a whale, it is actually the largest dolphin in the world. The Orca and its smaller relatives, such as the False Killer Whale and the pilot whales, are frequently referred to as "blackfish." Several authorities recognize these cetaceans as a separate family, but based on anatomical similarities, they are best classified as delphinids.

Striped Dolphin

Porpoise Family (Phocoenidae)

Porpoises, which number only six species worldwide, are widely distributed in the world, and there is very little range overlap between species. Although they superficially resemble dolphins, porpoises have unique features that set them apart from the better-known delphinids. They do not have a distinct beak, and their heads are quite rounded in appearance. Their body shape is a bit more robust than the streamlined dolphins, and their flippers are typically small and stubby. Unlike dolphins, which have conical teeth for holding and biting prey, porpoises have flattened, spade-shaped teeth that function to slice their prey.

Beaked Whale Family (Ziphiidae)

Beaked whales represent a large but poorly understood family of whales. They mainly inhabit deep ocean waters where people rarely visit, so accounts of their habits and behaviours are few. Some species of beaked whales have never been seen alive and are known only from individuals found dead on the shore or pulled in by fishing nets. There are 21 known species, but unrecorded beaked whale species may exist.

The ziphiids are referred to as beaked whales because all of them have a prominent snout. Males have two or four teeth that erupt on their lower jaw, either in the front or along the sides. Females and juveniles usually do not have erupted teeth of any sort. The lower jaws of the males and mature females may slope upward in the middle, giving the appearance that the "lip" is wrapping around the upper jaw. The teeth of the males further exaggerate this arch, and in some species the two teeth wrap over the upper jaw. This feature greatly reduces the ability of the whale to open its jaws, but beaked whales are believed to feed by sucking their prey into their mouth.

Cuvier's Beaked Whale

Dwarf Sperm Whale Family (Kogiidae) and Sperm Whale Family (Physeteridae)

Two families worldwide represent the sperm whales. The famous Sperm Whale, subject of Herman Melville's book *Moby Dick*, belongs to the family Physeteridae. The smaller sperm whales, in the family Kogiidae, are poorly understood, and very little information exists about their habits and natural history.

The most distinguishing feature of a sperm whale is its extremely large head. The largest of all, the head of a male Sperm Whale may be as much as one-third of the length of its body. The exact function of the large head is still under much debate. Some people think its serves to focus the echolocation clicks when the whale searches for food in very deep and dark water. Other theories suggest that the head, full of high-quality spermaceti oil, controls the buoyancy of the whale as it rises and dives through the water.

Pygmy Sperm Whale

Beluga

Delphinapterus leucas

In the far northern waters of the world, the elegant white Beluga thrives among the blue-white icebergs. This whale is unmistakable, but passing boats can overlook it amid the floating chunks of ice.

Often nicknamed "sea canary" by sailors, this loquacious whale has a vast repertoire of whistles, warbles, squeaks, clucks and squeals unlike that of any other cetacean in the world. A Beluga produces these sounds in the air passages in its head, and they are probably modified and amplified in the "melon," or forehead. Belugas seem to have the unique ability to bulge or shrink their melon at will, which may account for the large variety of sounds they produce. The melon of the Beluga, like that of other toothed whales, functions primarily for sound amplification and detection for echolocation. Given the sophistication of the Beluga's melon, the Beluga probably has one of the best sonar systems of any whale. A Beluga can navigate in water that is barely deep enough to cover its body, as well as in open ocean.

Despite many research efforts, we do not know the significance of the Beluga's calls. We know that certain sounds are associated with courtship and familial greetings, but whether these whales just chatter noisily or are actually communicating with language remains a mystery. In cases where a juvenile has stranded and must wait six hours for a new high tide—risking sunburn, dehydration and detection by a polar bear—the sounds made by the pod

RANGE: has a circumpolar distribution in the subarctic and high arctic; movements follow the formation and retreat of seasonal ice.

OTHER NAMES: White Whale, Sea Canary.

STATUS: endangered (COSEWIC) in some areas; locally common in the subarctic.

ADULT LENGTH: up to 5.5 m; average 4 m.

ADULT WEIGHT: up to 1600 kg; average 820 kg.

BIRTH LENGTH: about 1.5 m.

BIRTH WEIGHT: about 82 kg.

An anomalous population of Belugas survives in the St. Lawrence and Saguenay rivers. It is believed that these Belugas remained there after the northward retreat of sea ice following the last Ice Age. This population is declining, and the whales suffer ill-health from the terrible pollutants that contaminate their bodies. When a St. Lawrence Beluga dies, its body must be removed and treated like toxic waste because of the toxins stored in its fat.

members in the water are distinctive. In one case where a stranded juvenile survived the tide and returned to the bay, the cacophony of squeaks and trills from its pod were distinctly different from their earlier sounds.

DESCRIPTION: An adult Beluga is unmistakable, with its white body. It molts annually, and just prior to molting, its old skin appears yellow. After the molt, the new skin is gleaming white. A Beluga does not turn white until it is about 5 or 6 years old, and as a juvenile it is dark brown, slate

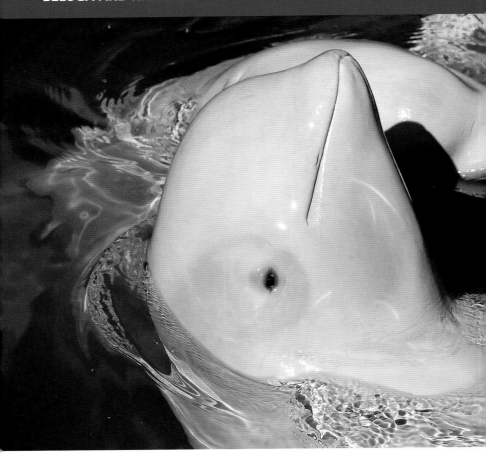

blue or pinkish grey. The Beluga has a small, bulbous head with a very short but prominent beak. The flippers may curl upward slightly, and so may the tips of the flukes. The trailing edge of the flukes and the dorsal ridge may have a brown tinge. The flukes are notched in the middle and may appear convex in shape. Despite its robust appearance, the Beluga is an extremely flexible creature. Its neck vertebrae are not fused like in most other whales, so it can move and nod its head around as it watches its surroundings. Its body is also flexible, and it can twist and turn as it dives underwater. Males are generally larger than females.

BLOW: The blow of the Beluga is low and steamy and can only be seen on calm, cool days. The loud, puffing sound that accompanies the blow is often more detectable than the blow itself.

OTHER DISPLAYS: Belugas do not breach, but they frequently spy-hop and lob-tail. When they rise above the surface, they turn their heads left and right as they survey their surroundings. Because Belugas

GROUP SIZE: Belugas are commonly seen in small groups of 5 to 20 members, but at certain times of the year, hundreds or even a few thousand of these whales may gather together at river deltas.

FEEDING: The Beluga feeds on a variety of sea creatures, such as squid, fish, molluscs and other invertebrates. Although it may feed near the surface, it frequently dives deep into the ocean, sometimes to a depth of 800 m, where it is presumably feeding on deepwater creatures such as squid.

REPRODUCTION: When a female is ready to give birth, she swims into deltaic calving waters that are 1 or 2 degrees warmer than the open sea. Nevertheless, the shock received to a newborn must be great because it goes from a warm environment inside its mother to the cold surrounding water. The calf stays with its mother for at least 2 years, and sometimes as long as 4 years if the mother does not get pregnant immediately after the calf is weaned. Normally, a female gives birth every 2 to 3 years. Peak calving period is in late summer, mating is in early spring or summer, and gestation is about 14 months. Males become sexually mature when they are at least 8 years old and females when they are 4 to 7 years old.

are gleaming white, their activities underwater are visible, provided they are not too deep. When they are molting, they roll and rub themselves on the bottom. In shallow river deltas, where hundreds of Belugas can be seen together, their frolicking and playful behaviour is visible. In many cases, Belugas underwater near a whale watching boat will turn upside-down while swimming so they can look up at the human observers on the deck above them.

SIMILAR SPECIES: The Narwhal (p. 76) is darker in colour, and most have a tusk; the Risso's Dolphin (p. 94) is dark grey, but older individuals whiten from scarring.

Narwhal

Narwhal

Monodon monoceros

DESCRIPTION: The extraordinary Narwhal has one of the most distinguishing characteristics of all mammals: a "horn" like that of a unicorn. This horn is really a tooth, so it is more aptly called a tusk. Perhaps 1 in 500 Narwhals has 2 tusks. Normally only the males have a tusk, though females sometimes have one as well. The body is mainly greyish white with dark grey or brown spots that are concentrated over the back and head. Some Narwhals may be completely dark over their backs, though most become lighter with age. Like the Beluga, the Narwhal lacks a dorsal fin, but it has a dorsal ridge about 5 cm high. The lack of a dorsal fin is believed to be an adaptation to the icy environs; sometimes these whales use their backs to break through ice that forms over their breathing holes. The pectoral fins measure 30–40 cm long, and width of the tail flukes is 1–1.2 m.

BLOW: The blow is small and puffy, and the gasping sound is easily heard.

OTHER DISPLAYS: Narwhals may spend several minutes at breathing holes with their head and tusk out of the water. They are very vocal, and their clicks, squeaks and whistles are used daily.

GROUP SIZE: Narwhals normally live in small pods of 3 to 8 individuals, though groups of 20 or more may form. On rare occasions there have been reports of hundreds and even thousands of individuals congregating in open waters. The reason for such large meetings is not understood.

FEEDING: Narwhals feed primarily on squid, fish, crustaceans and molluscs. The vertebrae in their necks are not fused, allowing them a great range of motion as they hunt. Because they have only a few teeth, they likely catch their prey by suction and swallow it whole.

REPRODUCTION: The calf is a dark brownish grey colour, and it lightens and gains spots as it matures. The calf may be nursed for as long as 20 months, though usually less. Mating tends to be from March to May, and after a gestation of about 15 months 1 calf is born, in July or August. Narwhals may live more than 50 years.

RANGE: found in arctic waters, from Canada, past Greenland and Scandinavia to Siberia.

OTHER NAMES: Unicorn Whale.

STATUS: threatened (IUCN).

ADULT LENGTH (WITHOUT TUSK): up to 4.7 m; average 4.3 m.

TUSK LENGTH: up to 3 m; average 2.6 m.

ADULT WEIGHT: up to 1600 kg; average 1200 kg.

BIRTH LENGTH: 1.5–1.7 m.

BIRTH WEIGHT: about 80 kg.

TOOTHED WHALES

SIMILAR SPECIES: The Beluga (p. 72) is similar in shape but is all white and lacks the tusk.

Beluga

Bottlenose Dolphin

Tursiops truncatus

The familiar Bottlenose Dolphin is rivalled only by the Orca as the most recognized cetacean species in the world. This fame is owed in part to aquarium performances and TV shows (such as *Flipper*), but also to the species' natural curiosity and friendliness toward humans. All over the world, the Bottlenose Dolphin is reported to hobnob with swimmers and perform acrobatics for admiring whale watchers. Of all cetaceans, this species is one of the best studied, especially in the fields of behavioural ecology, intelligence and communication.

The issue of non-human intelligence is loaded with misconceptions and biases. The main problem is that we have no guaranteed means of assessing intelligence in other animals. We can study their behaviour and conduct performance tests, but there always seems to be a margin of doubt and error in every method we use. Nevertheless, it is clear that Bottlenose Dolphins are among the most intelligent of all mammals.

A close look at the brain of a dolphin reveals information about the potential intelligence of the creature. Second only to humans, a dolphin's brain is very large for its body size—a ratio called the "encephalization quotient." The only other creature to exhibit such a high ratio is the chimpanzee; on performance tests, however, Bottlenose Dolphins routinely figure problems out much faster than chimpanzees.

When a test animal must activate switches to give correct answers, for example, chimpanzees routinely make random pokes at the switches before figuring out their purpose. Dolphins manage to trigger switches correctly with few, if any, random attempts. Another characteristic of a Bottlenose Dolphin's brain is the extremely well-developed cerebral cortex. The cerebral cortex is involved with the precise echo-location used by dolphins, but this part of the brain

RANGE: found around the world in tropical waters and in some temperate waters, but distribution is not continuous; favours bays and oceanic islands; considered occasional in Atlantic Canada.

OTHER NAMES: Bottle-nosed Dolphin, Atlantic/Pacific Bottlenose Dolphin, Grey Porpoise, Grey Dolphin, Cowfish.

STATUS: common.

ADULT LENGTH: up to almost 4 m; average 3 m.

ADULT WEIGHT: up to 650 kg; average 200 kg.

BIRTH LENGTH: about 1.1 m.

BIRTH WEIGHT: about 23 kg.

that they may even be distinct species. As well as subspecies, there appear to be two different varieties: the small and slender "inshore" dolphins, and the larger and more robust "offshore" dolphins. These two varieties exhibit social and behavioural differences. Offshore Bottlenose Dolphins appear to undergo slight seasonal migrations. Bottlenose Dolphins are rare in Canadian waters, and records are known only from the Atlantic, not the Pacific. The waters near Nova Scotia are the very northern limit of their range along eastern North America.

is also responsible for intellect, thought, language and memory.

Worldwide, three different subspecies of Bottlenose Dolphins have been described: *T.t. truncatus* in the Atlantic, *T.t. gilli* in the Pacific and *T.t. aduncus* in the Indian Ocean. Some researchers argue

DESCRIPTION: This robust dolphin is mainly bluish grey, with subtle markings on the face, such as bands of darker grey from the eye to the flipper or from the eye to the top of the rostrum. The facial markings vary greatly between individuals and populations. Normally the undersides are light grey or whitish. The forehead is rounded, and there is a crease separating the short but prominent beak from the rest of the head. The dorsal fin is falcate and sometimes slightly hooked at the tip. This dolphin's flippers are dark coloured on both sides, and they are broad at the base but taper to a long, slender point. The tail stock is thick, giving the dolphin a powerful appearance. Its flukes are distinctly notched, with swept-back tips. Members of offshore groups tend to be more robust than those of inshore groups.

individuals rarely dive for longer than 5 minutes, but offshore dolphins may remain submerged for as long as 15 minutes.

GROUP SIZE: Group size can vary regionally and between populations. Offshore groups are larger, numbering up to 25 individuals, whereas inshore groups rarely number over 10. At times, up to 500 Bottlenose Dolphins have been sighted in open waters.

FEEDING: The Bottlenose Dolphin feeds on a surprising variety of creatures, such as fish, squid, octopus, eels, rays, shrimp, crabs and even small sharks. In some regions, this dolphin has been seen herding fish onto shore, following behind and grabbing the fish as they flop around on land. After consuming the fish, the dolphin slides or wriggles its way back into the water.

REPRODUCTION: Reproduction is well studied for this species. A female gives birth every 2 or 3 years. Gestation is 12 months, and nursing lasts 12 to 18 months. The age of first reproduction is not the same as the age of sexual maturity because social dynamics may influence mating. Sexual maturity may occur at 5 years (or later) for females, and at 10 or 11 years for males. The lifespan in the wild is 35 to 40 years.

BLOW: This dolphin does not make a distinct blow, but the sharp puffing sound is clearly audible at short range.

OTHER DISPLAYS: The Bottlenose Dolphin is famous for its acrobatics. It will frequently bow-ride and lob-tail, and when it breaches it often clears the water completely, sometimes with an added twist or somersault. Groups are highly active and play extensively at the surface. Inshore

SIMILAR SPECIES: The Risso's Dolphin (p. 94) has numerous scars over its body and does not have a prominent beak.

Risso's Dolphin

Striped Dolphin
Stenella coeruleoalba

DESCRIPTION: This streamlined dolphin is easy to recognize because of the distinct thin stripe running from its eye to the underside of its tail stock. The Striped Dolphin is grey over most of its back, light grey on its sides and white or pinkish underneath. The border between the dark and light grey colours forms a zigzag below the dorsal fin. The dorsal fin is curved, and both the fin and flippers are dark on both sides. The pale grey flukes are slightly concave and notched in the middle. The beak is prominent and dark coloured.

BLOW: This dolphin does not have a visible blow, but if you are close enough, the sound of its breathing is audible.

OTHER DISPLAYS: The Striped Dolphin is highly acrobatic, and it breaches the water to heights up to 7 m. It may turn somersaults in the air or turn tail spins, re-entering the water in

a graceful dive. This dolphin can "porpoise" through the water upside-down.

GROUP SIZE: Striped Dolphins are commonly found in herds of 100 to 500 members. At times, up to 3000 of them have been seen together.

FEEDING: This dolphin's primary diet is small to medium-sized fish and squid.

REPRODUCTION: Successful mating can occur in either summer or winter. After a gestation period of 12 to 13 months, the female gives birth to 1 calf.

RANGE: found in warm-temperate, sub-tropical and tropical waters around the world.

STATUS: insufficient data worldwide; locally common in some areas.

ADULT LENGTH: up to 2.7 m; average 2.1 m.

ADULT WEIGHT: up to 160 kg; average 120 kg.

BIRTH LENGTH: 90 cm–1.1 m.

BIRTH WEIGHT: unknown.

SIMILAR SPECIES: The Short-beaked Saddleback Dolphin (p. 84) has a distinct yellowish patch behind its eye; the Atlantic White-sided Dolphin (p. 88) has a tricoloured body and a bicoloured beak; the White-beaked Dolphin (p. 92) has an entirely white beak.

Short-beaked Saddleback Dolphin

Females are sexually mature at about 90 percent of their adult length. Males, though they are sexually mature when they are about 9 years old, are not socially mature enough to mate until they are 16 years old.

Atlantic White-sided Dolphin

White-beaked Dolphin

83

Short-beaked Saddleback Dolphin

Delphinus delphis

More so than any other dolphin group, the saddleback dolphins seem to confound both taxonomists and biologists alike. At least 20 species have been proposed worldwide, as well as several subspecies. Officially, the group was recently split into two species: the Short-beaked Saddleback Dolphin (*D. delphis*) and the Long-beaked Saddleback Dolphin (*D. capensis*). As the names suggest, the latter has a longer beak than the former, and, in general, the Long-beaked Saddleback Dolphin has a longer and slightly slimmer body, more muted colouration and a thicker dark line from the lower jaw to the flipper than the Short-beaked Saddleback Dolphin. Although both species occur on the west coast of North America, only the Short-beaked is known to occur in the waters of Atlantic Canada. During summer and autumn, these dolphins can be found in shelf waters around Newfoundland and Nova Scotia.

Where they occur, Short-beaked Saddleback Dolphins are usually a very abundant species. They are also very sociable and are regularly seen with both Striped Dolphins (p. 82) and Risso's Dolphins (p. 94).

Like many other dolphins, saddleback dolphins are able to make an array of different sounds; they click, squeak and whistle, and they have a particularly high-pitched squeal that can even be heard from above the water. When large groups of saddleback dolphins are playing, they can be so loud and loquacious that

RANGE: widely distributed in warm-temperate, subtropical and tropical waters of the world.

OTHER NAMES: Short-beaked Common Dolphin, Common Dolphin, Criss-cross Dolphin.

STATUS: common.

ADULT LENGTH: up to 2.6 m; average 2 m.

ADULT WEIGHT: up to 140 kg; average 77 kg.

BIRTH LENGTH: about 75 cm.

BIRTH WEIGHT: unknown.

resting, they are alert for danger. Dolphins literally have the ability to sleep in halves: they are able to rest one eye while the other stays alert. Their brain also rests one hemisphere at a time, allowing for a constant state of awareness.

Unfortunately, one danger to which dolphins are oblivious is fishing nets, and a significant number of they are heard long before they are seen. If the herd is startled, they bunch tightly together for safety. Saddleback dolphins are very wary of Orcas (p. 98) and sharks, and if the alarm is called they flee at full speed directly away from the threat. Even when they are

saddleback dolphins are killed each year by fishing activities. Saddleback dolphins are at high risk of getting caught in nets because in some waters, they associate closely with yellowfin tuna.

DESCRIPTION: This small to mid-sized dolphin is easy to identify because of its unique colouration. On each side, beginning behind the eye, there is an arching, tan-coloured patch. This patch can be quite yellowish, but on some animals it is a dull muddy grey. The tail stock has a light grey area, also in an arch, and where the grey meets the yellowish patch on the side, there is a distinct criss-crossing pattern. The back is mainly dark brown or bluish black, and the undersides are whitish. The beak is dark coloured and sometimes white-tipped, and there are streaks of white or grey around the face. A dark circle always surrounds the eye, and a dark streak runs from the lower jaw to the flipper. The broad flippers are dark on both sides, as are the pointed flukes. The triangular dorsal fin is centrally located, and often the centre is a lighter grey than the rim. The flippers, dorsal fin and flukes all trail backward, giving the dolphin a streamlined appearance.

BLOW: The blow of a saddleback dolphin is not visible. At close range, however, the

Long-beaked Saddleback Dolphin

Short-beaked Saddleback Dolphin

FEEDING: Saddleback dolphins feed mainly on small schooling fish, such as herring, anchovies and sardines. A group of dolphins typically herds the fish into a tight ball and then begins feeding. Such cooperative strategies are used by many species of dolphins. Feeding dolphins can attract seabirds to an area because the birds benefit from the herded fish. Some people speculate that the reverse may be true too; a flock of feeding seabirds indicates the whereabouts of fish and might attract dolphins to the area.

REPRODUCTION: The reproductive ages and lengths of saddleback dolphins can vary between different regions and sub-species, but generally females are sexually mature when they are 1.8 m long, and males when they are 2 m long. Mating and calving can occur at any time of the year, and gestation takes 11 to 12 months. The social structure of a group might influence courtship and mating.

SIMILAR SPECIES: The Striped Dolphin (p. 82) has a stripe from its eye to under its tail stock; the Atlantic White-sided Dolphin (p. 88) has a tricoloured body and a bicoloured beak; the White-beaked Dolphin (p. 92) has an entirely white beak.

sound of its breathing can be heard when it is in mid-leap.

OTHER DISPLAYS: Saddleback dolphins are exceptional acrobats, and they frolic and play in noisy displays. They may leap high out of the water and fall gracefully back in with little splash. They frequently bow-ride, and other displays include flipper slaps, jaw slaps and lob-tailing.

GROUP SIZE: Perhaps the most numerous dolphins in the world, the saddleback dolphins have a world population that may well be in the millions. Group size is extremely variable, from a few dozen individuals to over 10,000. In Atlantic Canada, group size tends to be fewer than 100 dolphins, but groups of up to 3000 have formed in good feeding waters.

Striped Dolphin

Atlantic White-sided Dolphin

Atlantic White-sided Dolphin

Lagenorhynchus acutus

This large and colourful dolphin inhabits cool to temperate waters in the North Atlantic. Common around the Maritimes and Newfoundland, the Atlantic White-sided Dolphin can be seen in pods of a couple of dozen individuals. Large pods, numbering about 60, are sometimes found near the shores of Newfoundland. Occasionally, pods numbering several hundred dolphins are reported. For unknown reasons, this dolphin seems to strand more frequently than others in the region. Sometimes individuals strand, and sometimes groups of several dozen or even a hundred or more are reported stranded. These strandings may occur at any time of the year, and despite the efforts of researchers and volunteers, few of the stranded dolphins are saved.

Another common dolphin in the same region is the Short-beaked Saddleback Dolphin (p. 84), and these two species are often misidentified. The Short-beaked Saddleback Dolphin has the yellow side streak to the front of the dorsal fin, rather than to the rear. Both species are playful and quick to bow-ride. Atlantic White-sided Dolphins are sometimes even seen riding the bow waves of large whales. These dolphins, and other members of the same genus, are often referred to as "lags," a diminutive of their scientific name. As a group, these dolphins are not only acrobatic but also very sociable. Together they surf ocean waves, catch wakes, ride bow waves and "porpoise" in unison.

RANGE: found in subarctic waters of the North Atlantic: western edge of range extends from Greenland to New England; eastern edge stretches from western Norway to Great Britain.

STATUS: stable.

ADULT LENGTH: up to 2.8 m; average 2.4 m.

ADULT WEIGHT: up to 230 kg; average 200 kg.

BIRTH LENGTH: about 1 m.

BIRTH WEIGHT: about 20 kg.

dolphins are considered an open ocean species, but they come to near shore waters in spring in search of mackerel.

The total population of Atlantic White-sided Dolphins is only about 300,000 individuals. Fewer than 1000 of these dolphins are hunted every year, but many more accidental deaths from fishing nets also occur every year.

Atlantic White-sided Dolphins tend to prefer cool, low salinity waters. Although these dolphins are not strongly migratory, there is movement between inshore and offshore waters in response to food availability. Normally, these

DESCRIPTION: The Atlantic White-sided Dolphin actually appears to be tri-coloured; the belly and lower sides are white, the sides are grey, and the back is dark grey or black. Its facial markings are quite distinct; it has a black eye ring and a bicoloured beak, black above and grey below. A faint grey stripe may connect the leading edge of the flipper with the eye ring or rear margin of the lower jaw. There is a diagnostic lateral yellow stripe to the rear of the dorsal fin, sometimes with a leading portion of white. The fins are all strongly pointed; the flippers are about 30 cm in length, the dorsal fin may be up to 50 cm in height, and the tail flukes are up to 60 cm across. Females are a bit smaller than males.

BLOW: There is no discernible blow, but they often clear the water every 10 to 15 seconds to breathe. Sometimes they swim just below the surface, so their head cuts the surface of the water to make a spray that is often mistaken for a blow. When they are wary or moving slowly, they will rise just enough to expose their blowhole and then curl back under.

OTHER DISPLAYS: Playful and acrobatic, Atlantic White-sided Dolphins are known to breach high out of the water and bow-ride with fast boats. They often swim just

TOOTHED WHALES

FEEDING: Lanternfish, herring, mackerel, squid, smelt, hake and shrimp appear to make up the bulk of the diet. Atlantic White-sided Dolphins are not considered deep divers; although they can be found in waters up to 300 m deep, they do not dive to the bottom and rarely stay underwater for more than 4 minutes. Sometimes they cooperate in their efforts to surround and attack schools of fish.

REPRODUCTION: Females give birth to 1 calf every 2 years. The peak calving period is in June and July but extends from May to August. Females mate again when the calf is about 1 year old, and the gestation is about 11 months. Calves are weaned when they are 1½ years old. Sexual maturity is reached after 6 years of age. These dolphins usually live 25 to 30 years.

SIMILAR SPECIES: The Short-beaked Saddleback Dolphin (p. 84) has a yellow streak on its side behind its eye and a distinct criss-crossing pattern on its side below the dorsal fin; the White-beaked Dolphin (p. 92) has an entirely white beak; the Striped Dolphin (p. 82) has a stripe from its eye to under its tail stock.

Short-beaked
Saddleback Dolphin

White-beaked Dolphin

below the surface of the water, creating a spray off their head and dorsal fin.

GROUP SIZE: Pods of dolphins numbering several dozen are most common. Large pods of several hundred sometimes form, especially if they are following large whales that are feeding. Social dynamics also influence pod segregation. There is a strong tendency for young, sexually immature dolphins to form their own pod, much like teenagers hanging out with each other.

White-beaked Dolphin

Lagenorhynchus albirostris

DESCRIPTION: This robust dolphin is dark grey or nearly black, with indistinct white patches on the beak, sides, belly and back behind the dorsal fin. There is considerable variation in the colouration between individuals. The belly, "chin" and beak are white. The melon is dark grey or black, and the eye is in the dark colouration. The white beak contrasts sharply with the dark melon. The dorsal fin is long, narrow and strongly falcate on the trailing edge.

BLOW: White-beaked Dolphins make a small, slightly splashy blow as though they begin exhaling before their blowhole is clear of the water. The sound of their blow is audible at close range.

OTHER DISPLAYS: These dolphins are fond of bow-riding, and they frequently make high jumps out of the water. White-beaked Dolphins are known to accompany Fin Whales (p. 58) and Humpback Whales (p. 60) to good feeding areas.

GROUP SIZE: Group size varies from 5 to 50 members, though about 30 is the most common. Like other dolphin species, large gatherings of 1000 individuals or more sometimes form. The reason for these large gatherings is not known. These dolphins are sometimes encountered in mixed groups with Bottlenose (p. 78) and Atlantic White-sided (p. 88) dolphins.

FEEDING: White-beaked Dolphins are found in shelf and offshore waters, but they seem to prefer water that is no more than

TOOTHED WHALES

RANGE: found in the North Atlantic, from the Barents Sea to Cape Cod.

STATUS: stable.

ADULT LENGTH: up to 3.2 m; average 2.7 m.

ADULT WEIGHT: up to 350 kg; average 220 kg.

BIRTH LENGTH: about 1.2 m.

BIRTH WEIGHT: about 40 kg.

the ages of 7 and 12 years old. Mating and calving occur in summer. Females give birth to 1 calf after an 11-month gestation. Their lifespan is not known, but one individual was found to be 37 years old.

200 m deep. Their primary food is schooling fish such as haddock, cod, hake and whiting. Squid and crustaceans, primarily crabs, are also eaten. Seasonal fluctuations in their preferred prey species influence their inshore/offshore movement.

REPRODUCTION: White-beaked Dolphins become physically and socially mature enough to reproduce somewhere between

SIMILAR SPECIES: The Atlantic White-sided Dolphin (p. 88) has a tricoloured body and a bicoloured beak; the Short-beaked Saddleback Dolphin (p. 84) has a yellowish patch behind its eye; the Striped Dolphin (p. 82) has a stripe from its eye to under its tail stock.

Atlantic White-sided Dolphin

93

Risso's Dolphin

Grampus griseus

DESCRIPTION: Unlike almost every other dolphin or whale, the Risso's Dolphin becomes so heavily scarred that old individuals can appear almost white. The scars result from teeth scratches incurred during sparring matches with each other or from the hooks on the tentacles of squid. This dolphin has a stout body and a blunt head. It has an unmistakably tall dorsal fin, long, sickle-shaped flippers and pointed, trailing flukes. Males are generally larger than females.

BLOW: The Risso's Dolphin does not make a visible blow, but the sound of its breathing is audible if the animal is close.

OTHER DISPLAYS: These dolphins are not as acrobatic as the smaller dolphins, but younger animals may breach fully out of the water. They are also seen spy-hopping, lob-tailing and flipper-slapping. Although Risso's Dolphins rarely bow-ride, they often surf in waves and wakes.

GROUP SIZE: Risso's Dolphins are regularly seen in groups of 3 to 50 individuals. Some groups can be as large as 1000, especially in food-rich waters. These dolphins sometimes associate with Atlantic White-sided Dolphins (p. 88).

FEEDING: In deep water, these agile dolphins feed primarily on squid, though some medium-sized fish are also eaten.

RANGE: found in deep tropical and temperate waters throughout the world; avoids cold polar waters.

STATUS: common.

ADULT LENGTH: up to 4 m; average 3 m.

ADULT WEIGHT: up to 500 kg; average 400 kg.

BIRTH LENGTH: 1.2–1.5 m.

BIRTH WEIGHT: unknown.

REPRODUCTION: Mating occurs primarily in spring, though the exact timing varies among different populations. Females give birth to 1 calf, usually in summer, after a gestation of 13 to 14 months. Both sexes are sexually mature when they are about 2.6 m long.

SIMILAR SPECIES: The Bottlenose Dolphin (p. 78) lacks the heavy scarring and has a more distinct beak; the Pygmy Sperm Whale (p. 116) and the Dwarf Sperm Whale (p. 118) have underslung lower jaws.

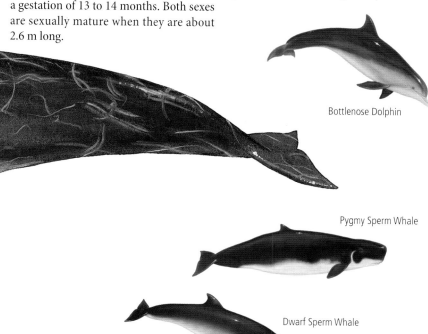

Bottlenose Dolphin

Pygmy Sperm Whale

Dwarf Sperm Whale

Long-finned Pilot Whale

Globicephala melas

DESCRIPTION: The Long-finned Pilot Whale is dark grey or black, with a signature anchor patch on the chest. The anchor patch is long and narrow and often continues to a white patch on the lower belly. Some individuals have a grey saddle patch behind the dorsal fin. Its long, pointed flippers and stumpy dorsal fin have a strongly swept-back appearance. The tail stock is thick, dwarfing the narrow tail flukes. Its melon is bulbous and often extends forward of the tip of the indistinct beak.

BLOW: This whale makes a strong but low, bushy blow that is sometimes visible.

OTHER DISPLAYS: Pilot whales engage in a variety of behaviours at the surface. They spy-hop, breach, log, lob-tail and "porpoise" through the water. Before a dive they show their tail flukes. This species is known for mass strandings, which usually result in numerous deaths. They are very social whales, and if one member of a group has stranded, the others appear to come to help but often end up stranding as well. The initial cause of the strandings is not known, but researchers theorize that the whales' echolocation is disrupted by shallow coastlines.

GROUP SIZE: Pods are tight and usually have 10 to 20 members, but these small pods are often part of a larger, loose group of over 100 individuals. Gatherings of several hundred pilot whales sometimes form, but for unknown reasons. These pilot whales often mix with Bottlenose (p. 78) and Atlantic White-sided (p. 88) dolphins.

RANGE: two distinct populations known; in the North Atlantic, ranges from Iceland to South Carolina.

OTHER NAMES: Pothead Whale, Blackfish.

STATUS: probably stable.

ADULT LENGTH: up to 7.6 m; average 6.7 m.

ADULT WEIGHT: up to 2300 kg; average 1700 kg.

BIRTH LENGTH: about 1.8 m.

BIRTH WEIGHT: about 75 kg.

go as long as 6 years between calves. Males are sexually mature at 12 or 13 years old.

FEEDING: Long-finned Pilot Whales primarily feed on squid, but they will take medium-sized fish when available. They feed mainly at night, making dives that last about 18 minutes at depths of about 800 m.

SIMILAR SPECIES: The Risso's Dolphin (p. 94) is a similar shape but has heavy scarring over its head and body; the Orca (p. 98) is larger, has a taller dorsal fin and is distinctly black and white.

Risso's Dolphin

REPRODUCTION: Mating and calving peak in the summer months, and females give birth to 1 calf after a gestation of 12 to 16 months. Nursing lasts 1½ to 3½ years. Females become sexually mature when they are about 8 years old, and they may

Orca

Orcinus orca

The Orca, also known as the Killer Whale, with its striking colours and intelligent eyes, has fascinated humans for centuries. Long revered by the indigenous peoples of North America, the Orca is now an icon for such concerns as biodiversity protection and contact with non-human intelligence. Images of this white-and-black giant can be found on everything from coffee cups to international conservation documents.

The Orca lives in every ocean of the world, from the cold polar seas to the warm equatorial waters, and it is one of the most widely distributed mammals on Earth. Uncontested as a top predator in the oceans, the Orca feeds on a wider variety of creatures than any other whale. It is regarded as an intelligent yet fearsome creature—it is the lion that rules the seas.

Studies indicate that there are three distinct types of Orca: "transients," "residents" and "offshores." The three kinds are distinguishable by appearance and behaviour, but the differences are subtle. Transient Orcas tend to be larger than residents, and they have taller, straighter dorsal fins. The transients live in smaller pods, from one to seven individuals, and they have

large home ranges; resident Orcas have seasonally small ranges and travel along predictable routes. Transients are most likely to feed on other sea mammals, they dive for up to 15 minutes, they make erratic direction changes while travelling, and they do not vocalize as much as residents. Resident Orcas feed mainly on fish, are

RANGE: found in all the world's oceans and most adjoining seas; the most widespread of all whales.

OTHER NAMES: Killer Whale.

STATUS: vulnerable; locally stable.

ADULT LENGTH: up to 9.8 m; average 8.5 m.

ADULT WEIGHT: up to 10,000 kg; average 6800 kg.

BIRTH LENGTH: 1.8–2.4 m.

BIRTH WEIGHT: about 180 kg.

highly vocal and rarely dive for longer than three or four minutes. Offshore Orcas resemble the residents in appearance, but they usually live farther out at sea. As well, offshore Orcas tend to travel in groups of up to 100 individuals. Much more research is needed to accurately describe the offshore Orcas. At this time, only the transients have been found in Atlantic Canada. Recent research, however, indicates that the number of Orcas in Newfoundland and Labrador is increasing, and preliminary findings suggest that

some of these Orcas demonstrate characteristics of residents.

Orcas have never been hunted heavily by humans. Some hunting has occurred in the past several decades, but it has not threatened the total population. One form of hunting that has taken many Orcas and their close cousins, the Bottlenose Dolphins (p. 78), is live hunting. Orcas are taken from the wild and introduced into the world aquarium trade, where they are expected to learn and perform tricks for the public. The capture of these animals for this purpose has caused much controversy, mainly because many people consider cetaceans to be extremely intelligent animals and think that keeping them in an aquarium is unjust. Much of what we have learned about cetacean intelligence and biology, however, has come from aquarium studies, and this knowledge helps us to better understand and protect whales in the wild.

DESCRIPTION: The Orca is unmistakable: its body is black, its undersides and lower jaw are white, there are white patches behind the eyes and on its sides, its large flippers are paddle-shaped and its dorsal fin is tall and triangular. The dorsal fin varies in shape and size from whale to whale, and it often bears scars and nicks. Old males may have a fin as tall as 1.8 m, and the fin of some old individuals is wavy when seen straight on. Females have a smaller, more curved dorsal fin than males. Behind the dorsal fin there is often a uniquely shaped grey or purplish "saddle." Scientists and whale watchers rely on these varying dorsal fin and saddle characteristics to identify individual whales. An Orca's eye is located below and in front of the white facial spot. The snout tapers to a rounded point. The flukes are dark on top and whitish below, and they have pointed tips, concave trailing edges and a distinct notch in the middle. Males are much larger than females.

Male

Female

FEEDING: Orcas feed on a wider variety of animals than any other whale, partly because of their global distribution. Several hundred animal species are potential prey to these top predators of the sea, including, but not limited to, seals, other whales and dolphins, dugongs, fish, sea turtles and birds. Even land mammals may be eaten—there are records of pods killing and eating moose and caribou that swim across narrow channels and rivers in British Columbia and Alaska.

REPRODUCTION: Mating probably occurs between individuals of a pod, but because "super-pods" occasionally form, paternity is almost impossible to ascertain without genetic analysis. Males reach maturity when they are about 5.8 m long, and females when they are about 4.9 m long. Winter appears to be the peak calving period, and gestation is believed to take 12 to 16 months.

SIMILAR SPECIES: The Long-finned Pilot Whale (p. 96) lacks the distinct black and white marking and has a shorter dorsal fin.

BLOW: In cool air, the Orca makes a low, bushy blow.

OTHER DISPLAYS: Orcas are extremely acrobatic whales for their size. They are inquisitive and often approach boats, apparently to get a better look at the humans on board. They are often seen breaching clear out of the water, lobtailing, flipper-slapping, logging and spy-hopping. They may speed-swim, or "porpoise," with their entire body leaving the water at each breath.

GROUP SIZE: Orcas usually travel in pods of 3 to 25 individuals. Some social gatherings may attract several pods at a time.

Long-finned Pilot Whale

Harbour Porpoise

Phocoena phocoena

The little Harbour Porpoise is the most widespread member of its family. It favours coastal waters such as estuaries, shallow bays and tidal channels, and it has even been seen short distances up rivers. It is rarely found in waters deeper than 300 m and seems to prefer water no deeper than 200 m. In Atlantic Canada, sightings are common in water less than 60 m deep.

In the past, this porpoise was a familiar sight to boaters and sailors of coastal waters, but its population is declining. In some regions, alarming numbers of Harbour Porpoises have washed up on shorelines either dead or dying. Although the reasons are not clear, many scientists suspect that high levels of toxins and pollutants impair the immune systems of these and other cetaceans, which makes them more susceptible to life-threatening diseases.

Drowning deaths are another main reason why Harbour Porpoises are declining. Because of this porpoise's feeding habits, it is frequently caught in bottom-set gill nets, a kind of net that sits deep in the water like a curtain attached to the bottom. Almost every

RANGE: found in cold-temperate and subarctic waters of the Northern Hemisphere.

OTHER NAMES: Common Porpoise, Puffing Porpoise.

STATUS: declining.

ADULT LENGTH: up to 2 m; average 1.5 m.

ADULT WEIGHT: up to 68 kg; average 59 kg.

BIRTH LENGTH: 65–90 cm.

BIRTH WEIGHT: about 5 kg.

The solution to this problem is not easy, but leading researchers have been working on ways to warn animals, particularly porpoises, where the nets are. Some sounds repulse Harbour Porpoises, and now a device called a "pinger" can be specially made and fitted to the nets. The pinger

kind of deep net can trap and drown a cetacean, but the most sinister nets are the ones that have been thrown away or lost by fishermen. An untended net catches numerous cetaceans, sea turtles, fish and other sea creatures until it is so heavy that it sinks to the bottom.

emits a sound that the porpoises do not like, resulting in the porpoises steering clear of the net. In the future, devices of this kind may help save the lives of thousands of porpoises and other cetaceans.

DESCRIPTION: This small porpoise is the smallest cetacean in the region. It is mainly dark or slate grey over the back, fading to white underneath. In some individuals the colour change is gradual, but in others the change is well defined, especially on the tail stock. Even on one individual, the colour pattern may not be the same from one side to the other. The face is small, the head tapers gently and the mouth angles slightly upward. This porpoise has black "lips," and 1 or 2 black streaks extend back to its all-black flippers. The dorsal fin and flukes are black as well. The flukes are pointed slightly backward, and they are notched in the middle.

Upon close examination, you can see little bumps, or tubercles, on the leading edges of the dorsal fin and flippers.

BLOW: Although Harbour Porpoises are difficult to observe because they rarely show much of themselves abovewater, they make a remarkable sound when they breathe. When a Harbour Porpoise breaks the surface, it makes a quick sneezing sound, which has earned it the nickname "Puffing Porpoise."

OTHER DISPLAYS: Like other porpoises, the Harbour Porpoise shows little of itself abovewater. It rarely performs acrobatics

TOOTHED WHALES

GROUP SIZE: Harbour Porpoises usually live in small groups of 2 to 5 individuals. Some groups have up to 15 members, and good feeding waters can attract from 50 to several hundred porpoises.

FEEDING: Harbour Porpoises feed in mid-water or on the bottom, and their main foods include small schooling fish, such as anchovies or herring. They rarely venture into water more than 200 m deep.

REPRODUCTION: Both male and female Harbour Porpoises mature sexually between the ages of 3 and 4. Mating usually occurs in early summer, and calving is 11 months later. The newborns are dull brown in colour, and for the first few hours they have birth lines or creases circumscribing their bodies. This species is not long-lived; most individuals die before they are 10 years old.

SIMILAR SPECIES: The larger Atlantic White-sided Dolphin (p. 88) has a distinct tricoloured pattern; the larger White-beaked Dolphin (p. 92) has more distinct markings and a larger dorsal fin.

Atlantic White-sided Dolphin

White-beaked Dolphin

like dolphins do, and it is not as fast or active as a dolphin. Only its comical sneezing sound attracts the attention of whale watchers. Harbour Porpoises do not like intruders, however, and if they are uncomfortable and want to hide they will lie silently and motionlessly just below the surface of the water. This behaviour also occurs at night, and it probably helps them remain undetected by predators. On rare occasions, Harbour Porpoises have been seen bow-riding. When they swim quickly, they may "porpoise" in and out of the water.

Cuvier's Beaked Whale

Ziphius cavirostris

DESCRIPTION: This medium-sized whale has a highly variable colour range that includes cream, beige, brown and purplish or reddish black. The colour pattern is swirled and blotchy, and most individuals have spots and scars along their sides and undersides. The head is triangular, with an indistinct beak and 2 small teeth on the protruding lower jaw. The flippers are small and close to the head. The dorsal fin is small and close to the tail. The flukes are pointed, only slightly notched in the middle and broad—they measure almost as much as a quarter of the length of the body. Females are generally larger than males.

BLOW: The blow is usually invisible, but it may be seen after a long dive. It is low and bushy, and it usually points forward and to the left.

OTHER DISPLAYS: This beaked whale breaches infrequently, rising vertically and completely out of the water and falling ungracefully back in. It usually avoids boats and whale watchers, but there are a few notable cases where inquisitive individuals have approached boats.

GROUP SIZE: When solitary Cuvier's Beaked Whales are seen, they are usually old males. Normally, these whales form groups of 2 to 10 members, but pods as large as 25 have been recorded.

FEEDING: Cuvier's Beaked Whales make deep dives of 20 to 40 minutes to feed on deep-sea fish and squid. They are rarely seen close to land.

RANGE: found throughout the world, in all seas except cold polar waters; the most widespread member of its family and probably the most common; known in Nova Scotia from Sable Island.

OTHER NAMES: Goose-beaked Whale, Cuvier's Whale.

STATUS: insufficiently known.

ADULT LENGTH: up to 7 m; average 6.1 m.

ADULT WEIGHT: up to 3200 kg; average 2300 kg.

BIRTH LENGTH: 2–2.9 m.

BIRTH WEIGHT: about 250 kg.

REPRODUCTION: Sexual maturity for both males and females is reached at about 75 percent of the adult length. The peak periods for mating and calving are unknown.

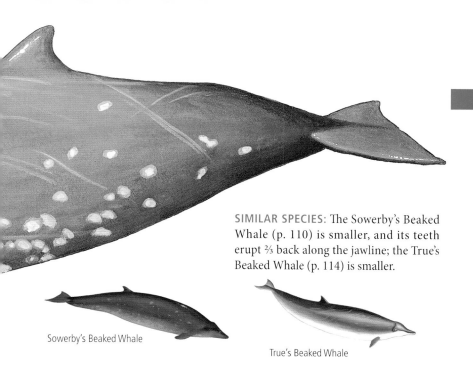

SIMILAR SPECIES: The Sowerby's Beaked Whale (p. 110) is smaller, and its teeth erupt ⅔ back along the jawline; the True's Beaked Whale (p. 114) is smaller.

Sowerby's Beaked Whale

True's Beaked Whale

North Atlantic Bottlenose Whale

Hyperoodon ampullatus

DESCRIPTION: These large beaked whales are usually grey, olive or brown in colour. Their sides are lighter and the belly is pale grey or white. Sometimes the colour is blotchy or swirly over the back. Both sexes have a pronounced melon, though it is somewhat smaller in females. There are 2 small, conical teeth at the tip of the lower jaw. The strongly falcate dorsal fin is 30–40 cm tall and is located ⅔ of the way down the length of the dorsum. Their tail flukes lack the notch in the centre. Males are about 1 m longer than females.

BLOW: When visible, the low, bushy blow is angled slightly forward.

OTHER DISPLAYS: This whale has been known to approach and circle slow-moving boats, sometimes even for hours. Lob-tailing and breaching are infrequent behaviours. Unlike most other whales, they do not commonly show their flukes before a deep dive.

GROUP SIZE: These whales are usually found in groups of 4 to 10 individuals, though it is not uncommon for 25 to 30 to be seen together.

FEEDING: North Atlantic Bottlenose Whales feed primarily on squid. Fish, cuttlefish and bottom-dwelling invertebrates such as sea stars and sea cucumbers are also consumed. Like other beaked whales, they feed by sucking their prey into their mouths.

REPRODUCTION: Between April and June, a female gives birth to 1 calf after a 12-month gestation. The calf

RANGE: inhabits most of the North Atlantic; although a deepwater species, it has been seen in the shelf waters of Atlantic Canada and sometimes ventures several kilometres into broken ice in subarctic zones; best-known population found in waters over the large submarine canyon known as the Gully, just off Nova Scotia.

OTHER NAMES: Northern Bottlenose Whale, Bottlehead.

STATUS: unknown.

ADULT LENGTH: up to 10 m; average 9 m.

ADULT WEIGHT: up to 7500 kg; average 6650 kg.

BIRTH LENGTH: about 3.5 m.

BIRTH WEIGHT: unknown.

is weaned at 1 year old and reaches maturity at 7 to 9 years old. These whales are known to live for more than 35 years.

SIMILAR SPECIES: All of the other beaked whales in the region (pp. 106–115) are much smaller. Even a juvenile North Atlantic Bottlenose Whale is distinct because of its pronounced melon.

Sowerby's Beaked Whale

Mesoplodon bidens

DESCRIPTION: Sowerby's Beaked Whales are generally bluish grey or charcoal grey in colour, with lighter undersides and belly. There are often scars from cookie-cutter sharks along their sides, giving them a mottled appearance. Their snout is tapered, and males have a slightly arched lower jaw with 2 conical teeth, 1 on each side about ⅔ back along the jawline. The teeth of females do not erupt, and their jawline is straight. The melon is only a slight bulge on the forehead, and it is more pronounced in males. The falcate dorsal fin is located quite far back, and the tail flukes lack a central notch.

BLOW: The blow is small and inconspicuous, even in cool weather.

OTHER DISPLAYS: These whales are known to breach, leaving the water at steep angles. Sometimes they clear the water completely before splashing back in. Occasional strandings are reported.

GROUP SIZE: Sowerby's Beaked Whales form small groups of 3 to 10 individuals.

FEEDING: This species feeds by suction and preys mainly on squid and some fish. It favours deep waters past the shelf, but it is known to visit and feed in waters over the deep submarine canyon known as the Gully off the coast of Nova Scotia. Some stranded, dead individuals were found to have swallowed plastic items, which likely caused or contributed to their death. Plastics, especially plastic bags, resemble the squid on which they feed. Other beaked whales are similarly affected.

RANGE: inhabits waters beyond the shelf edge in the North Atlantic from Massachusetts to Labrador to Norway.

OTHER NAMES: North Atlantic Beaked Whale, North Sea Beaked Whale.

STATUS: unknown.

ADULT LENGTH: up to 5.5 m; average 5.2 m.

ADULT WEIGHT: up to 1300 kg; average 1200 kg.

BIRTH LENGTH: 2.4–2.7 m.

BIRTH WEIGHT: about 185 kg.

REPRODUCTION: Little is known of the reproduction of these whales, but females are estimated to reach maturity at about 7 years old. Females give birth to 1 calf probably every 2 to 3 years.

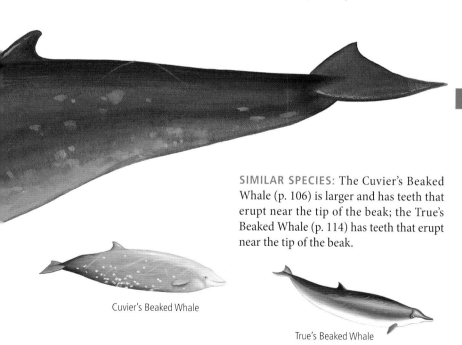

SIMILAR SPECIES: The Cuvier's Beaked Whale (p. 106) is larger and has teeth that erupt near the tip of the beak; the True's Beaked Whale (p. 114) has teeth that erupt near the tip of the beak.

Cuvier's Beaked Whale

True's Beaked Whale

Blainville's Beaked Whale

Mesoplodon densirostris

DESCRIPTION: This species is slate grey or bluish over the back, and it has pale undersides. The body may have extensive blotches and scars, giving it a mottled appearance. Perhaps the most distinguishing feature of this whale is the male's 2 teeth, which are quite large. They erupt from the lower jaw, which arches upward around the upper jaw, and, because the forehead is flattened, the tips of the teeth are often higher than the top surface of the snout. The female also has an arched lower jaw, but her teeth do not erupt and are not visible. The flippers are small, the dorsal fin is triangular and somewhat falcate, and the tail flukes are slender and swept backward. The peculiar Latin name (and an alternate common name) of this species refers to its dense bones. When this whale was first described, a sample of bone from the jaw was found to be of very high density. The

species has since been discovered to have the densest bones in the animal kingdom.

BLOW: This whale makes a small, inconspicuous blow that is directed forward. The best chance to see its blow is on a calm, cool day.

OTHER DISPLAYS: These whales are not acrobatic, and the extent of their surface behaviour is breathing and resting. When breathing before a deep dive, a Blainville's Beaked Whale will surface several times during a period of 20 to 45 minutes. The last time it surfaces before a deep dive, the forward roll of its dive sequence will be strongly arched.

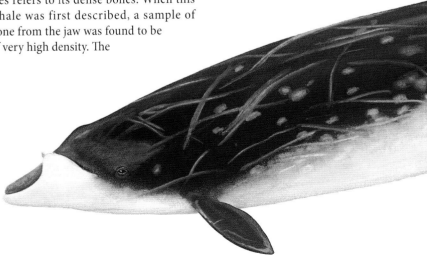

RANGE: found in warm-temperate waters around the world; distribution probably not continuous; population in the North Atlantic not well documented.

OTHER NAMES: Dense Beaked Whale, Tropical Beaked Whale, Atlantic Beaked Whale.

STATUS: insufficiently known.

ADULT LENGTH: up to 6.1 m; average 5.2 m.

ADULT WEIGHT: up to 1100 kg; average 900 kg.

BIRTH LENGTH: 1.8–2.6 m.

BIRTH WEIGHT: about 60 kg.

GROUP SIZE: These beaked whales usually live singly or in small groups of up to 6 members. Sometimes groups as large as 12 are seen.

FEEDING: Little is known about this whale's habits, but it probably feeds on squid and deepwater fish.

REPRODUCTION: Average age of sexual maturity is thought to be 8 or 9 years, but little else is known about this whale's reproductive habits.

SIMILAR SPECIES: The other beaked whales in the region (pp. 106–115) lack the strongly arched lower jaw.

True's Beaked Whale

Mesoplodon mirus

DESCRIPTION: The True's Beaked Whale is mainly dark grey or brown, with lighter sides and a pale, nearly white belly. Some individuals may have light patches around and behind the eye, and sometimes on the tail stock as well. Cookiecutter shark bite scars are common on older individuals, and long, scratchy scars may be seen on the backs of males. These are probably inflicted by other males during dominance fights in the mating season. The beak is relatively short, and the jawline is only slightly curved. A mature male has 2 teeth that erupt close to the tip of the beak. The melon bulges slightly between the beak and the blowhole. Its Latin name *mirus* means "wonderful" and was given to the whale by Frederick True, who was excited by his discovery of this new species. Further studies may reveal that the two apparently separate populations of True's Beaked Whales are actually distinct species.

BLOW: The blow is small and inconspicuous, even in cool weather.

OTHER DISPLAYS: When surfacing, True's Beaked Whales may show their entire beak. These whales have a low profile and have rarely been seen alive, and breaching is the only display that has been observed. Anecdotal evidence suggests that an injured individual is tended by at least one of its group members, a trait also described in other beaked whales.

GROUP SIZE: The most common group size appears to be 3 members, but single individuals have been encountered. Probably groups of more than 3 occur as well.

FEEDING: Like other members of its genus, the True's Beaked Whale feeds on

RANGE: two populations: one in the Atlantic from Nova Scotia to the Bahamas; the other in the Indian Ocean between South Africa and Australia.

OTHER NAMES: Wonderful Beaked Whale.

STATUS: unknown.

ADULT LENGTH: up to 5.4 m; average 4.8 m.

ADULT WEIGHT: up to 1400 kg; average 1100 kg.

BIRTH LENGTH: 2–2.5 m.

BIRTH WEIGHT: about 135 kg.

TOOTHED WHALES

deepwater squid and some fish. Although this is a deepwater species that feeds on deepwater prey, individuals have been sighted in shelf waters.

REPRODUCTION: Like other beaked whales in this family, females probably give birth to 1 calf every 2 to 3 years. Nothing is known of gestation and nursing periods, and the details of mating and birthing remain a mystery.

SIMILAR SPECIES: The Sowerby's Beaked Whale (p. 110) has teeth that erupt ⅔ back along the jawline; the Cuvier's Beaked Whale (p. 106) is larger.

Cuvier's Beaked Whale

Sowerby's Beaked Whale

Pygmy Sperm Whale

Kogia breviceps

DESCRIPTION: The overall body colour is slate blue, dark grey or even brownish, and the undersides are nearly white. Like its close relative, the Dwarf Sperm Whale (p. 118), this small whale is almost shark-like in appearance. It has a protruding snout and an underslung lower jaw, and many individuals have a streak behind the eye that resembles a gill slit. The blowhole is on top of the head and is displaced slightly to the left. The dorsal fin is tiny, slender and curved, and the flippers are broad and almond-shaped. The tail flukes are convex and notched, with distinctly pointed tips.

BLOW: These whales make small, inconspicuous blows that are visible only on clear, calm days and at close range.

OTHER DISPLAYS: When they surface to breathe, Pygmy Sperm Whales are very inconspicuous, and they usually drop out of sight immediately. These whales may occasionally breach, and they typically fall back into the water with little grace. They sometimes release a cloud of dark intestinal fluid that probably serves to either distract intruders or confuse prey, or both.

GROUP SIZE: Pygmy Sperm Whales live in small groups of 3 to 6 members. On rare occasions they have been observed singly or in groups as large as 10 individuals.

FEEDING: Pygmy Sperm Whales feed mainly in deep water, catching such creatures as squid, fish and some crustaceans.

RANGE: widespread in deep tropical, subtropical and temperate waters; known in Nova Scotia from Sable Island.

OTHER NAMES: Lesser Sperm Whale, Lesser Cachalot, Short-headed Whale.

STATUS: insufficiently known.

ADULT LENGTH: up to 3.7 m; average 3 m.

ADULT WEIGHT: up to 410 kg; average 350 kg.

BIRTH LENGTH: about 1.2 m.

BIRTH WEIGHT: about 55 kg.

REPRODUCTION: Length at sexual maturity is believed to be about 2.7 m for Pygmy Sperm Whales. Calving and mating may occur year-round, but there is little accurate data for this species.

SIMILAR SPECIES: The Dwarf Sperm Whale (p. 118) has a larger dorsal fin and a more pointed snout; the Risso's Dolphin (p. 94) has distinct scarring over its head and body.

Dwarf Sperm Whale

Risso's Dolphin

Dwarf Sperm Whale

Kogia sima

DESCRIPTION: This unusual whale resembles a slightly fat shark. Its snout is short and squarish, and its mouth is tiny and underslung. There is a white streak behind the eye that resembles a gill slit on a shark. Overall, the body is dark or bluish grey, with lighter undersides. The flippers are short and broad, and the dorsal fin is pointed and has a concave trailing edge. The flukes are broad and pointed, and they are notched in the middle. The blowhole is set above the eye and is slightly displaced to the left.

BLOW: The Dwarf Sperm Whale does not make a distinct blow.

OTHER DISPLAYS: When this whale rises to breathe, it does not roll forward into a dive like other whales; instead, it takes a quick breath and then simply drops out of sight. It may be seen resting at the surface, and it occasionally breaches—rising vertically out of the water and splashing back in haphazardly. When startled,

it may release a cloud of dark intestinal fluid that presumably distracts an intruder while it dives. These clouds are probably also released to confuse prey.

GROUP SIZE: Dwarf Sperm Whales travel alone or in pairs. On occasion, they have been seen in groups of up to 10 individuals.

FEEDING: This whale has a small mouth and presumably eats small creatures. Its primary foods are thought to be cuttlefish, squid and other fish.

REPRODUCTION: The gestation period for this whale is about 9 months,

RANGE: seen in a number of locations throughout deep temperate, sub-tropical and tropical waters in both the Northern and Southern hemispheres; known in Nova Scotia from Sable Island.

STATUS: insufficiently known; probably stable.

ADULT LENGTH: up to 2.7 m; average 2.4 m.

ADULT WEIGHT: up to 280 kg; average 200 kg.

BIRTH LENGTH: about 1 m.

BIRTH WEIGHT: 40–50 kg.

TOOTHED WHALES

and calving is at its peak during the summer months. Both sexes reach maturity when they are 75 to 80 percent of their adult length.

SIMILAR SPECIES: The Pygmy Sperm Whale (p. 116) has a smaller dorsal fin and a blunt snout; the Risso's Dolphin (p. 94) has distinct scarring over its head and body.

Pygmy Sperm Whale

Risso's Dolphin

Sperm Whale

Physeter macrocephalus

The famous Sperm Whale is a definite record-breaker in the world of mammals. It is easily the deepest-diving mammal on Earth, and it can hold its breath for more than two hours. Sperm Whales seem not to have a maximum diving depth—greater and greater dives keep being discovered. The restricting factor appears to be the time without oxygen, rather than the enormous pressure on the body. At 3200 m, which is believed to be the deepest recorded dive, the pressure on the body is a staggering 317 atmospheres, yet Sperm Whales are still able to function.

The Sperm Whale's biggest adaptation to surviving these pressures is that before it dives, it removes the air from its lungs to help minimize the difference in pressure between its body cavities and the surrounding water. Because the whale's body, like ours, is mainly water, it resists compression.

The mammoth head of the Sperm Whale is filled with spermaceti, an oil that may function to regulate the whale's buoyancy as it dives and surfaces. The other proposed theory is that the spermaceti serves to magnify or focus the whale's sound emission during echolocation. Perhaps the spermaceti performs both of these functions for the whale. Females have dramatically smaller heads than males, but the reason for this difference is not clearly understood. Females also dive deeply and rely on

DIVE SEQUENCE

RANGE: found in deep waters world-wide; although widespread, distribution is probably patchy.

OTHER NAMES: Cachalot, Anvil-headed Whale.

STATUS: vulnerable (IUCN); locally stable in some waters.

ADULT LENGTH: up to 21 m; average 15 m.

ADULT WEIGHT: up to 53,000 kg; average 32,000 kg.

BIRTH LENGTH: about 4 m.

BIRTH WEIGHT: about 900 kg.

TOOTHED WHALES

DESCRIPTION: The Sperm Whale is easy to recognize because of its extremely large head and distinctive features. The head is as much as ⅓ of the total body length. It is narrow when seen from above and rectangular when seen from the side. A male has a much larger and more rectangular head than a female. The

echolocation, so perhaps the larger head of the male serves another purpose.

Sperm Whales are present all year in deep waters of Atlantic Canada, though they are sometimes found in shallower waters in this region, too. Despite their presence, however, they are not reliably seen. Some tour operators may have current information on their whereabouts.

eyes are relatively small and inconspicuous. The mouth and tip of the snout may be white or light grey, and scarring may be obvious. The slightly raised blowhole is at the end of the snout, and it is displaced to the left. The overall body colour is brown, grey or nearly black, though the undersides are often lighter. The stubby flippers and broad, triangular tail flukes are dark on both sides, but scarring may lighten the edges. The trailing edge of the flukes is sometimes scalloped, and such variations in the tail are used by researchers to identify individuals. Instead of a true dorsal fin, the Sperm Whale has a distinct hump or knuckle where the fin would be. Several smaller knuckles continue down the dorsal ridge to the tail. The skin appears "pruney" from behind the eye to the tail stock. Males are much larger than females.

BLOW: Because the blowhole of the Sperm Whale is at the tip of the snout and displaced to the left, the blow sprays forward and to the left. No other whale makes a blow like this, so even from afar a Sperm Whale can be readily identified.

Diving

thousands of Sperm Whales have been reported.

FEEDING: The ability of the Sperm Whale to feed at great depths is unsurpassed by any other mammal. One of the deepest recorded dives is from two Sperm Whales that were believed to have reached 3200 m, where they had consumed bottom-dwelling sharks. The main foods eaten by Sperm Whales are squid and giant squid, octopus, large fish and sharks. Sperm Whales locate their food in the darkness of deep water by using their extremely sophisticated echolocation.

REPRODUCTION: Although males are sexually mature when they are about 10 years old, they are unlikely to mate for several more years. Females are sexually mature when they are 8 to 12 years old. Mating usually occurs in late winter or early spring, and single calves are born in summer or fall, following a gestation period of 14 to 15 months. The young may nurse for several years, even after they start eating solid food.

SIMILAR SPECIES: No other whale has a head as large as that of a Sperm Whale. The Humpback Whale (p. 60) has a similar dive sequence, but its knobby head is unmistakable.

OTHER DISPLAYS: Sperm Whales, especially juveniles, may breach and lob-tail. When they return from a deep dive, they breathe at the surface 30 to 40 times before diving again. The first breath is very loud and explosive, but the subsequent breaths are quieter. Between dives, the whales usually stay at the surface for about 15 minutes, but sometimes they will remain near the surface for as long as an hour.

GROUP SIZE: Sperm Whales usually live in groups of 2 to 25 animals. Nursery colonies of females and young number 12 to 30 individuals, and bachelor colonies of many young males are also common. At times, assemblages of hundreds or even

Humpback Whale

Seals and Otters

During a trip on the waters of Atlantic Canada, you may see several mammals other than whales, such as seals and otters. Although these other marine mammals are adapted to life in the ocean, they are unlike whales in that they are able to come ashore at any time. All seals, sea lions and otters are members of the order Carnivora, as are dogs, cats, bears and weasels, among others.

Outwardly, all the seals look similar, and they were once classified in their own order, Pinnipedia, meaning "fin feet." Further study revealed that seal-like mammals are actually a good example of convergent evolution, where creatures of different origins look or function similarly because of comparable adaptations to a common problem. There are two distinct lineages of seals: the eared seals (and their later offshoot, the Walrus), which likely share a common ancestor with bears, and the hair seals, which are descendants of an ancestral member of the weasel family. Eared seals are not found in Atlantic Canada, but they are common along Canada's west coast. Despite having different lineages, all seals and sea lions are still frequently referred to as pinnipeds.

Walrus Family (Odobenidae)

The Walrus—the only member of this family—is an unmistakable inhabitant of cold polar and subpolar waters. Like the eared seals, the Walrus is able to rotate its hindlimbs under its body to help it move on land. Unlike most other seals, the Walrus spends much of the day hauled out on rocky shores or ice packs. The Walrus has two features that are similar to the hair seals: all of its digits have claws, and it has no external ears. Perhaps the most distinguishing feature of the Walrus is its tusks. Both sexes have tusks, though males tend to have longer ones.

Walrus

Hair Seal Family (Phocidae)

The hair seals are also referred to as either the "earless" seals or the "true" seals. As the former name suggests, they have no visible external ears. The best way to distinguish these seals is by body shape. The hindflippers of hair seals are permanently pointed backward—they are unable to rotate their hindlimbs forward to help support their body weight when they are on land. As a result, when hair seals are on land they move with clumsy undulations of their bodies. Once in the water, hair seals are graceful, lithe swimmers capable of high speeds and rapid turns. Their forelimbs are small compared to those of eared seals, but the flippers are strong enough that the seal can hold itself upright and tread water at the surface. Members of this family all have hair on their flippers and claws on all five digits of each flipper.

Ringed Seal

Otter Subfamily (Lutrinae)

Otters are a subgroup of the weasel family (Mustelidae), which includes terrestrial carnivores such as minks, weasels, badgers and martens. There are two otters in North America: the Sea Otter and the Northern River Otter. The Sea Otter, which only lives on the west coast, was once heavily hunted for its thick fur. The Northern River Otter is similar to the Sea Otter, except that it is smaller and slimmer and has a longer tail. Although the Northern River Otter typically inhabits fresh water and is not strictly a marine mammal, it can be seen in some coastal waters.

Northern River Otter

Walrus

Odobenus rosmarus

Truly one of a kind, the Walrus is the sole member of its family. It most likely arose from an ancestral eared seal, but after 7 million years of adaptation, the Walrus is unlike any other living seal. The Walrus's unique tusks, which grow throughout an individual's life, are its most distinguishing feature. The tusks are modified teeth, and they are coated in enamel when they first erupt. Over time, the enamel wears off, leaving a tusk of pure ivory.

RANGE: Atlantic race found from Labrador through Baffin Bay and into Hudson Bay.

STATUS: stable.

ADULT LENGTH: males up to 3.7 m; females up to 2.9 m.

ADULT WEIGHT: males up to 1500 kg; females up to 910 kg.

TUSK LENGTH: males up to 1 m; females up to 36 cm.

The exploitation of Walruses for their ivory was once extensive, but it has nearly been stopped now, thanks to the Marine Mammal Regulations (MMR) in Canada and the Marine Mammal Protection Act in the U.S. These two acts protect Walruses and other marine mammals in North America from game hunting and exploitation. Only Inuit, who have traditional links to this animal, continue to hunt the Walrus. Inuit use all parts of the animal: the meat is eaten; the skin is used as leather for clothing or covers for boats; and the bones and tusks are used in sculptures and carvings that bring additional revenue into the communities.

There are two distinct Walrus races: the Pacific Walrus, which is the larger of the two, inhabits the region from the Chukchi Sea off northeastern Siberia to Alaska; the Atlantic Walrus lives in Hudson Bay and east to Greenland. Both races of Walrus live in groups of anywhere from a few dozen to up to 2000 individuals. The Atlantic Walrus numbers only about 20,000 individuals, and researchers have

noticed that the population is in decline. The reasons for the decline are not known.

Walruses are excellent swimmers that can reach speeds up to 24 km/h. They may sleep on land, but they also have the ability to sleep vertically in the water with their heads held up by inflated air sacs in the neck. When they dive for food, they can descend to 90 m deep, remaining underwater for as long as 30 minutes.

DESCRIPTION: Both bull and cow Walruses have tusks, but a cow's tusks are considerably shorter and more curved than a bull's. Walruses have very little hair over their bodies, and their skin colour varies from nearly white or pale pink to yellow, reddish or brownish. The hindflippers have nails on all 5 digits and can be rotated underneath so the walrus can "walk" on all fours on land. The foreflippers lack nails completely. The face is covered with about 400 whiskers, each up to 30 cm in length. Walruses have no visible tail.

HABITAT: Historically, Walruses may have inhabited more of the northern islands and rocky shores than they do now, but the impact of human hunting has pushed them farther into the arctic seas. Currently, they spend most of their time on pack ice over water that is usually about 18 m deep. The Atlantic Walrus is not migratory, and it prefers landfast ice that does not travel. Walruses spend more of their time basking than do other seals, usually on ice or rocky outcroppings.

FEEDING: Using its mouth like a powerful vacuum, the Walrus sucks molluscs out of their shells. Clams are the most common food, and a Walrus can polish off up to 6000 of the bivalves in 1 day. The Walrus is opportunistic, and it will feed on fish, crabs, shrimp, worms and a variety of other marine creatures.

REPRODUCTION: Although females reach sexual maturity as early as 4 years old, they generally do not start reproducing until they are about 8 years old. Males reach sexual maturity between ages 7 and 10, but they are not socially or physically mature enough to compete for mating opportunities until they are about 15 years old. Unlike other seals that usually mate each year, a female Walrus mates every 2 years. Gestation is 11 to 12 months, and the single newborn calf weighs 45–68 kg. The cow nurses her calf in the water in a vertical position. The calf remains with the mother and nurses from her for nearly 2 years. The mother separates from the calf before she has another baby.

SIMILAR SPECIES: All of the seals (pp. 130–147) in the same region are much smaller and lack tusks.

Harbour Seal

Phoca vitulina

The inquisitive Harbour Seal is a well-known resident of Atlantic Canada. This seal bespeckles rocky coastlines at almost any time of the day throughout the year. It basks onshore either alone or in groups numbering up to the thousands.

Although many Harbour Seals may bask on rocks together, they pay very little attention to their neighbours and seldom interact. During the pupping season, females with newborn pups may congregate in a "nursery" in shallow water where the pups can sleep. The pups and the females sleep underwater, rising occasionally for a breath. These nursery groups are not socially interactive—they are simply a precautionary measure against predators.

While most of the females and pups are sleeping, some are likely to be awake and watchful for danger. The same is true for hauled-out seals. Where several seals are together, the chances are good that there is always at least one individual awake and wary of approaching danger.

Harbour Seals tend to be cautious of humans, and if you approach them on land they are likely to dive immediately into the water. Many kayakers and boaters,

SEALS AND OTTERS

RANGE: found along the northern coasts of North America, Europe and Asia; inhabits the entire coast of Atlantic Canada.

OTHER NAMES: Common Seal.

STATUS: common.

ADULT LENGTH: 1.2–1.8 m.

ADULT WEIGHT: 50–140 kg.

Tracks

however, have enjoyed watching inquisitive individuals that approach their boats for a better look. This kind of encounter is controlled by the seal: if it wants to see you, it will come closer, and if it is afraid of you, it will leave. Approaching a seal that has attempted to flee can cause unnecessary stress to the animal.

When the tide is out at night, Harbour Seals sleep high and dry at favourite haul-out sites. They frequently rest with their head and rear flippers lifted above the rock they are sleeping on. During the day, they can sleep underwater in shallow coastal water by resting vertically just above the bottom. Young pups commonly rest in this manner. Harbour Seals can go without breathing for nearly 30 minutes, and although they sometimes wake up to breathe, they frequently rise to the surface, take a breath and then sink back to the bottom without waking.

DESCRIPTION: The Harbour Seal is typically dark grey or brownish grey, with light, blotchy spots or rings, but some individuals may have the reverse colour pattern—light grey or nearly white with dark spots. The undersides are generally lighter than the back. The outer coat is composed of stiff guard hairs about 1 cm long, which is the characteristic that gives seals of this family the name "hair seals."

The guard hairs cover an undercoat of sparse, curly hair, about 6 mm long, that helps provide insulation for the seal. Pups bear a spotted silvery or grey-brown coat at birth. The head is large, round and very dog-like, except that there are no visible ears. Each of the short foreflippers has long, narrow claws. Males are generally larger than females.

FEEDING: Harbour Seals feed primarily on fish, such as rockfish, cod, herring, flounder and salmon. To a lesser extent, they also feed on molluscs (such as clams, squid and octopus) and crustaceans (such as crabs, shrimp and crayfish). Newly weaned pups seem to consume more shrimp and molluscs than do adults. Adult Harbour Seals have been seen taking fish from nets, and some have even entered fish traps to feed and then easily departed.

REPRODUCTION: Gestation lasts 10 months, and females give birth to a single pup in pupping colonies from mid-April to July. The pups are weaned when they are 4 to 6 weeks old, after they have tripled their birth weight feeding on their mother's milk, which is more than 50 percent fat. Within a few days of weaning her pup, a female mates again. Harbour Seals become sexually mature anywhere from 3 to 7 years of age. Captive seals have lived for more than 35 years, but typical lifespans are 20 years for males and 30 years for females.

SIMILAR SPECIES: The Ringed Seal (p. 134) has a more regular pattern of rings instead of spots; the Harp Seal (p. 140) has a distinct harp pattern over its back; the Grey Seal (p. 138) is larger.

HABITAT: This near-shore seal is frequently found in bays and estuaries. Favoured haulout sites, which are traditionally used by many generations of Harbour Seals, commonly include intertidal sandbars, rocks and rocky shores. The Harbour Seal sometimes follows fish several hundred miles up major rivers, and there are even populations in some inland lakes—usually within 160 km of the coast.

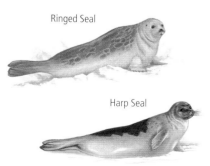

Ringed Seal

Harp Seal

Ringed Seal

Pusa hispida

Studies of the Ringed Seal have provided information not only about the biology of this small seal, but also about the biogeological history of the continent. By identifying the variety of sea creatures on which Ringed Seals feed, the faunal picture of the northern seas can be partially described, both in modern times and historically.

Fossils of Ringed Seals that have been discovered, some near Ottawa, give clues to the geology and habitat of the area more than 10,000 years ago. Ringed Seals are known to live in cold, saltwater habitats, so we can infer that similar conditions existed at one time where these fossils were found. More importantly, we know that other animals—the prey species of Ringed Seals—must have also lived in the region. In this way, the fossil history of the Ringed Seal can provide good information about our continent since the last Ice Age.

When a Ringed Seal dives for crustaceans, it can reach a maximum depth of about 90 m. It can stay under for up to 18 minutes, though a dive usually lasts five minutes or less. Unlike its cousin the Bearded Seal (p. 142), the Ringed Seal cannot tolerate the pressure at great sea

SEALS AND OTTERS

RANGE: found in the polar seas from Point Barrow, Alaska, in the West to Labrador in the East.

STATUS: stable.

ADULT LENGTH: 1.2–1.7 m.

ADULT WEIGHT: 50–110 kg.

depths, nor can it tolerate being without air for much longer than 15 minutes. As a result, the Ringed Seal remains in relatively shallow areas, while the Bearded Seal occupies deeper waters.

Although it spends most of its time in the water, the Ringed Seal digs small chambers under the snow, but above the ice, where it rests when it needs to reoxygenate its blood after a long dive.

Sometimes, many seals are found together in chambers that are connected by short passageways.

Walruses (p. 126), sharks and Orcas (p. 98) are the biggest threats to the Ringed Seal in the water, while polar bears, arctic foxes and humans are the dangerous creatures on the ice. There is no place where this seal is truly safe, and it seems to know it—every minute or so a Ringed Seal lifts its head to scan its surroundings for danger. Even in its snowy den, this seal is watchful and ready to flee from a polar bear that has sniffed it out and dug through the snow to reach it. The arctic fox, which preys on the pups, is small enough to walk right into the den.

PCBs, DDT and other environmental contaminants are found in the blubber of Ringed Seals, and this contamination is known to reduce pregnancy rates. In some years of heavy contamination, the number of pregnant females dropped by

50 percent. In combination with heavy losses from predation, and from hunting in some areas, these low fertility rates may threaten the survival of some local Ringed Seal populations. Furthermore, recent studies suggest that the contamination is worse when there are more ice-free days in the year. With climate predictions for more ice-free days in the Arctic, the contaminant loads in seal blubber will likely increase.

DESCRIPTION: This little seal is one of the smallest aquatic carnivores. Its fur is variegated brown or even bluish black above and pale yellowish or grey below, with irregular doughnut-shaped rings of light-coloured fur on the sides and back. It has long whiskers and eyebrows, a short muzzle and dark eyes. Males are typically larger than females.

In deep water, their diet shifts to larger zooplankton, such as amphipods.

REPRODUCTION: A female typically mates annually, in April or early May, and gives birth to a single pup the following March, after 11 months of gestation. The Ringed Seal is unique among seals because of the maternal den it constructs under the snow. A pregnant female may hollow out a shallow chamber in the snow above a breathing hole, or she may use a natural snow cave. Maternal chambers are typically about 2 m in diameter and only 30–50 cm high. The young are born helpless, but with all their teeth, and covered in lanugo (the soft downy fur that is reminiscent of a teddy bear). A pup nurses for about 2 months. When its mother leaves the den to feed, the pup remains by itself and waits quietly. Some pups may stay near their mothers for the remainder of the year, while other pups may disperse soon after weaning.

SIMILAR SPECIES: The Harbour Seal (p. 130) has irregular spots and blotches; the Harp Seal (p. 140) has a distinct harp pattern over its back; the larger Grey Seal (p. 138) has a different range.

HABITAT: The Ringed Seal spends most of its life underwater in the northern polar seas. It maintains breathing holes under the ice by digging the ice away with its sharp claws. This seal usually stays under or near landfast ice, and it is seldom seen on shifting or broken ice floes.

FEEDING: In shallow water, these seals feed mainly on crustaceans and small fish.

Harbour Seal

Harp Seal

Grey Seal

Halichoerus grypus

DESCRIPTION: These medium-sized seals have a very straight profile and nostrils that are quite far apart. They are mainly silvery grey or brown, with darker spots and blotches. Older males may have heavy scarring around their necks. Males are as much as 30 percent larger than females. Grey Seals are extremely vocal, and, in addition to bleats and gurgling sounds, they sing eerie songs. Their combined voices sound like a group of school children pretending to be ghosts.

HABITAT: Grey Seals inhabit the North Atlantic, specifically coastal waters where they can hunt for benthic fish at depths of 70–100 m. There are haul-out sites and rookeries on both Atlantic shores. The largest breeding colony in the world is on Sable Island, just off the coast of Nova Scotia, and this protected colony is likely responsible for the increase of Grey Seals in New England.

FEEDING: Grey Seals feed on a wide variety of fish, especially benthic (bottom-dwelling) ones. Eels, cod, flatfish, herring and skates are commonly eaten, as well as octopus and lobster. These seals fast during the pupping and breeding season.

REPRODUCTION: Females come to shore in September, and pups are born from late September through November. Within a few weeks of giving birth, the female may mate again. Gestation is a little over 11 months, including a period of delayed

SEALS AND OTTERS

RANGE: found in coastal waters of Atlantic Canada and New England, Iceland, Great Britain, Scandinavia and northern Europe.

OTHER NAMES: Atlantic Seal, Horsehead Seal.

STATUS: stable, with some local increase.

ADULT LENGTH: males up to 2–2.7 m; females up to 1.6–2.2 m.

ADULT WEIGHT: males up to 240–320 kg; females up to 150–260 kg.

implantation. Pups are born with white, fuzzy lanugo. Pups weigh 14 kg at birth but grow very quickly because their mother's milk is about 60 percent fat. At about 1 month old, the pups shed their lanugo and develop their waterproof adult fur. Soon after, they head out to sea and feed for themselves. Grey Seals become sexually mature between 3 and 5 years old, and they can live for a long time; females up to 40 years and males up to 30 years.

SIMILAR SPECIES: The Harbour (p. 130), Harp (p. 140) and Ringed (p. 134) seals are smaller. The Bearded Seal (p. 142) is usually larger and more uniformly coloured and has a long, bristly "beard." The Hooded Seal (p. 146) is strongly spotted, and the male has an inflatable forehead sac.

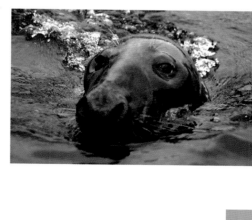

Harp Seal

Phoca groenlandica

DESCRIPTION: Silvery white or greyish overall, this seal gets its name from the dark wishbone- or harp-shaped patch of fur over its back. Some individuals never fully develop their harp pattern and have just spots or blotches. These individuals are called "Spotted Harps." The pups are covered in fuzzy white fur for their first 12 days.

HABITAT: During winter months, Harp Seals haul out on ice in arctic and subarctic waters, where they give birth and later mate. The rest of the year is spent at sea; the peak of summer finds them in high arctic seas near Ellesmere Island. When feeding, they prefer waters not more than 300 m deep.

FEEDING: Harp Seals regularly dive to depths of 150–200 m to find their prey. They consume many kinds of small fish, such as capelin, cod, herring, sculpin, halibut, redfish and plaice. In fact, they are known to eat more than 65 different kinds of fish and at least 70 kinds of invertebrates (such as crab, lobster and shrimp).

REPRODUCTION: Pups are born in rookeries on ice in late February or March. They are 80–90 cm long and have a fuzzy, yellow coat. After 2 or 3 days, the yellow coat is shed and the pup is covered in its famous white lanugo. The lanugo only lasts for 12 days, the period of the pup's most intense growth. The pups weigh about 10 kg when they are born, but they

RANGE: circumpolar; migrates between arctic and subarctic waters; in North America, winter range is around Atlantic Canada to as far south as New England; summer range can reach as far north as Ellesmere Island and west into northern Hudson Bay.

OTHER NAMES: Greenland Seal, Saddle-backed Seal, Jumping Seal.

STATUS: common.

ADULT LENGTH: 1.6–1.9 m.

ADULT WEIGHT: 85–180 kg.

are capable of putting on an astonishing 25 kg in their first 10 to 12 days. They require this fat to survive; they are weaned at day 12, but they cannot swim until they are at least 4 weeks old. During these initial weeks, their newly stored fat keeps them alive. After the white lanugo is shed, the pup has a silvery coat with spots for up to 4 years. Sexual maturity is sometime after 4 years, at which time the adult colour pattern is achieved. Females mate soon after giving birth, and males stay around the pupping colony for weeks to improve their chances of finding receptive females. Females have a delayed implantation of about 4 months, and their gestation is 7½ months, which results in pups being born at the same time every year.

SIMILAR SPECIES: Other seals (pp. 130–147) lack the harp pattern, and the Grey Seal (p. 138) is larger.

Bearded Seal

Erignathus barbatus

The Bearded Seal is perhaps the most vocal of all seals—what it lacks in its non-descript appearance, it easily makes up for with its repertoire of unusual and haunting calls. In spring, the male Bearded Seal sings melodious yet eerie songs beneath the ice. The songs can last for up to a minute, and they carry for a long distance underwater. To court a female, a bull hauls out on the ice and serenades the cows with his echoing, warbling calls.

Bearded Seals can dive to a maximum depth of about 200 m. Mammals that are not specialized for diving—such as humans—would suffer from the "bends" when descending to such depths and returning to the surface. The bends is a condition where nitrogen bubbles form in the blood as the pressure decreases: nitrogen already present in the blood may come out of solution, or expanding nitrogen from the lungs can transfer directly into the blood. This condition occurs when the body has adjusted to the great pressure underwater, and a rapid return to the surface reduces the pressure too quickly.

Extensive research has been conducted to determine how certain species of seals can dive unharmed to such great depths. It turns out that before a dive, the seals breathe air out of their lungs, rather than into their lungs. The air they do retain is

RANGE: inhabits the northern coastal waters and shallow arctic seas from Point Barrow, Alaska, to Labrador.

STATUS: stable.

ADULT LENGTH: 2–2.6 m.

ADULT WEIGHT: 250–360 kg.

held in their windpipe. The windpipe is more rigid than the lungs and can tolerate the pressure changes of the dive. This unique method prevents the bends from occurring.

When humans hold their breath, the increasing carbon dioxide levels in the blood trigger them to breathe again in a very short time. This trigger is greatly desensitized in seals, and they are able to postpone breathing for about 30 minutes. When a seal is underwater, its nostrils are closed and its heartbeat is slowed from the normal 100 beats a minute to about 10 beats a minute. During the dive, the muscles function mainly anaerobically, creating an oxygen debt in the body.

Seals store oxygen in their blood and in certain molecules of the muscle itself, and this stored oxygen is used, or "spent," during the dive. The longer the dive lasts, the greater the body's oxygen debt becomes. When the dive is over, the seal must rest and rebuild, or "pay back," the oxygen stores of its body. When a Bearded Seal is basking, it is not just enjoying the sun; it is allowing its body to slowly reoxygenate after a long dive.

DESCRIPTION: As its name suggests, this seal has a beard of long, flat bristles on either side of the muzzle. Other seals have whiskers, but none compare to the long, bristly beard of the Bearded Seal. Each long bristle is extremely sensitive, and together the bristles help the seal locate its favourite foods in the mucky sediment of the sea floor. The head of this large seal is noticeably small for its body size. The fur varies in colour from uniformly light brown to tawny golden to greyish. The front flippers are distinctively squarish, and the third digit is longer than all the rest. In a switch from many other pinnipeds, female Bearded Seals are slightly larger than males.

HABITAT: The Bearded Seal spends most of its time in the water of cold arctic seas. It primarily stays in water no deeper than 150 m because it dives to the bottom to feed. The Bearded Seal is only rarely seen

SEALS AND OTTERS

REPRODUCTION: In May, the mating season is marked by these normally solitary seals forming groups of up to 50 individuals. The males are marvelously vocal, and they emit warbling calls on the ice surface to serenade the females. Females are not vocal. Sometimes the bulls fight each other to establish hierarchy, but the dominant bulls do not form harems. A female gives birth on the ice to 1 young in April or May, after a gestation of about 11 months. The pup is well developed at birth and is nursed for no more than 18 days. The pup puts on blubber during this short nursing period and goes from weighing 32 kg at birth to about 90 kg by day 18, at which time the pup is weaned and the mother leaves.

SIMILAR SPECIES: The Grey Seal (p. 138) is usually smaller and has spotty or patchy markings. The Hooded Seal (p. 146) is strongly spotted, and the male has an inflatable forehead sac.

Grey Seal

Hooded Seal

on land—it prefers open water and rests on drift ice and ice floes. This seal is not migratory, but it does follow the seasonal movement of the ice.

FEEDING: Using its powerful claws and keenly sensitive whiskers, the Bearded Seal locates bottom-dwelling fish and shellfish to eat. Favourite foods include cod, sculpin, flounder, octopus and a variety of shellfish, including whelks and clams.

Hooded Seal

Cystophora cristata

DESCRIPTION: Adults are silvery grey with dark spots. The dark spots are more concentrated on the head and face, contributing to their "hooded" appearance. The male has an inflatable skin sac above the nostrils. During courtship, the male exhales air into this sac, which becomes larger with age. When the sac above the nose is not inflated, it looks like a loose hood. Males can also inflate the membrane between their nostrils, which then looks like a red balloon. Males develop their inflatable nasal sac at sexual maturity, sometime after they are 4 years old. Females are only half the size of males. Pups are fuzzy and bluish grey.

HABITAT: These seals make extensive migrations through arctic and subarctic waters. They haul out on ice twice a year, once for the pupping season and soon after to moult. Mostly they moult on ice, but in some parts of their range they may moult on rocky shorelines.

RANGE: found in the central and western North Atlantic.

OTHER NAMES: Crested Seal, Bladder Seal.

STATUS: declining.

ADULT LENGTH: males 2.3–2.9 m; females 2–2.3 m.

ADULT WEIGHT: males up to 435 kg; females up to 350 kg.

FEEDING: Hooded Seals feed on a wide variety of fish, molluscs and crustaceans. Their diet seems to vary regionally but mainly includes halibut, redfish, cod, capelin, herring, mussels, starfish, squid, shrimp and octopus. They feed at depths of 100–600 m.

are 5 to 8 days old. Their mother's milk is twice as rich in fat as whipping cream, so this short period of nursing is sufficient for a pup to double its weight—from 24 kg at birth to 47–50 kg before weaning. A few days after the pup is weaned, the male that has been "guarding" the female will mate with her in the water. The female has delayed implantation of about 3½ months, so her 8-month gestation means pups are born at the same time every year.

REPRODUCTION: In late winter, Hooded Seals gather in great numbers on the ice, where they give birth and later mate. Newborn pups are covered in a bluish grey lanugo and are nicknamed "bluebacks." Some pups are nursed for as little as 4 days, the shortest of any mammal. Usually pups are weaned when they

SIMILAR SPECIES: A Bearded Seal (p. 142) is a similar size but has a long, bristly "beard." A male Grey Seal (p. 138) can be as large as a Hooded Seal but lacks the "hood."

Bearded Seal

Northern River Otter

Lontra canadensis

Contrary to its name, the Northern River Otter is a year-round resident of coastal areas in Atlantic Canada, in addition to its regular inland habitats. Although there are no true Sea Otters (*Enhydra lutris*) on the east coast, there was once the Sea Mink (*Neovison macrodon*) that lived in New England and the Maritimes. The Sea Mink was prized for its thick coat and was hunted to extinction by 1890. The Northern River Otter was also hunted, but its much larger range and population buffered it from extinction. Today, the Northern River Otter lives throughout the coast, now largely free of the hunting pressures that decimated the Sea Mink population. The competitive fur trade played an important role in North America's early economy, but it resulted in the endangerment, extirpation and extinction of many species.

RANGE: range extends from Labrador to Texas on the east coast, and from the Bering Strait to northern California on the west coast.

STATUS: uncommon.

ADULT LENGTH: 1.1–1.4 m.

TAIL LENGTH: 30–50 cm.

ADULT WEIGHT: 4.5–14 kg.

The Northern River Otter has a well-deserved reputation for playfulness. Otters often amuse themselves by rolling, sliding, diving or "body surfing," and they may also push and balance floating sticks with their noses or drop and retrieve pebbles for minutes at a time. They seem particularly interested in playing on slippery surfaces—they leap onto snow or mud with their forelegs folded close to their bodies for a streamlined toboggan ride. Unlike most members of the weasel family, river otters are social animals, and they will frolic together in the water and take turns sliding down slippery rocks.

With their streamlined bodies, rudder-like tails, webbed toes and valved ears and nostrils, river otters are well adapted for life in the water. When they emerge from water to clamber over rocks, there is

Back footprint   Front footprint

Tracks

a distinct serpentine appearance to their movement. In the water they are lithe and efficient at catching prey. Although otters generally cruise along slowly in the water by paddling with all four feet, they can dart after prey with the ease of a seal whenever hunger strikes. When an otter swims quickly, it propels itself mainly with vertical undulations of its body, hindlegs and tail. Otters can hold their breath for as long as five minutes.

Because of all its activity, the Northern River Otter leaves many signs of its presence when it occupies an area. Slides are the most obvious indicator of a resident otter. Also, despite its penchant for life in the water, an otter always defecates on land. Its scat is simple to identify—it is always full of fish bones and scales.

A river otter may make extensive journeys across land, and although this animal looks clumsy on land, it can easily outrun a human, even with its humped, loping gait. On slippery surfaces, such as wet grass, snow or mud, the otter glides along, usually on its belly with its legs tucked either back or forward to help steer and push. On flat ground, slides are sometimes pitted with blurred footprints where the otter has given itself a push for momentum.

DESCRIPTION: This large, weasel-like carnivore has a dark brown back that looks black when it is wet. It is paler below, and the throat is often silver-grey. The head is broad and flattened, and it has small eyes, small ears and prominent, whitish whiskers. All 4 feet are webbed. The long tail is thick at the base and gradually tapers to the tip. Males are larger than females.

HABITAT: Northern River Otters may visit coastal areas for brief periods, or they may live at the coast year-round. They sometimes roam far from water, especially young males establishing new territories. When roaming, a river otter rests under roots or overhangs, in hollow logs, in the abandoned burrows of other mammals or in ledges on rocky outcroppings.

FEEDING: On the coast, river otters feed primarily on fish such as sculpin, gunnel and flatfish. Crabs and shellfish are eaten when available. Coastal river otters also occasionally eat small terrestrial animals such as mice, insects and earthworms.

REPRODUCTION: In coastal areas, the den is in a burrow or crevice away from the shore. The female bears a litter of 1 to 6 blind, fully furred young in March or April. The young are 140 g at birth. They first leave the den at 3 to 4 months, and they leave their parents at 6 to 7 months. River otters become sexually mature at 2 years. The mother breeds again soon after her litter is born, but delayed implantation of the embryos puts off the birth until the following spring.

SIMILAR SPECIES: The American Mink (*Neovison vison*) could be confused with a river otter, but although it sometimes lives in coastal marshes, it prefers freshwater habitats because its fur is not very tolerant of saltwater.

Glossary

AMPHIPOD: a shrimplike crustacean (e.g., krill) of the order Amphipoda that has a laterally compressed body; the primary food for many whale species

BALEEN: strands of keratin that hang in sheets from the upper jaw of whales in the suborder Mysticeta and are used to filter food from water

BENTHIC: dwelling at or near the bottom of a lake or ocean

BOW-RIDING: a behaviour seen in dolphins in which the animals swim in the bow waves of boats

BREACH: a whale display in which the animal rises vertically into the air, clearing the water's surface with almost all of its body before splashing back in

BULL: an adult male cetacean or pinniped

CALF: a baby cetacean

CALLOSITY: an area of skin that is hardened by growths of lumpy, keratinous material; commonly found on the head of a right whale

CETACEAN: a marine mammal of the order Cetacea, which encompasses all whale, dolphin and porpoise species

COLONY: a group of animals living together and interacting socially

COPEPOD: any of a large group of small marine and aquatic crustaceans, including amphipods; the primary food for many marine creatures

COW: an adult female cetacean or pinniped

Melon

Beak/Snout

Eye

DELPHINID: a member of the ocean dolphin family (Delphinidae)

DORSAL: pertaining to the back or spine (compare **VENTRAL**)

DORSUM: the back or dorsal region of the body

ECHOLOCATION: the detection of an object by emitting sound waves and interpreting the returning echoes, which are changed by bouncing off the object

ENCEPHALIZATION QUOTIENT (EQ): the ratio of an animal's brain weight to its body size; used as a measurement of the possible intelligence of an animal

ENDANGERED: facing imminent extirpation or extinction

EXTINCT: no longer in existence anywhere

EXTIRPATED: no longer found in a given geographic area but still in existence elsewhere in the world

FALCATE: curved or somewhat sickle-shaped

FLUKE: *n.* either of the lobes on a whale's tail; *v.* a whale behaviour in which the animal raises its tail above the water before diving

FUSIFORM: spindle-shaped; having an elongated body that tapers at both ends

GESTATION: the time of pregnancy, from conception to birth

KERATINOUS: referring to the material that composes hair, wool and nails in many mammals

KRILL: a general name to describe more than 80 species of small, shrimplike organisms that are eaten by numerous marine creatures

HABITAT: the environment in which an animal or plant lives

HOME RANGE: the total area through which an individual animal moves during its usual activities (compare **TERRITORY**)

LANUGO: the fine, soft hair that covers the body of newborn mammals

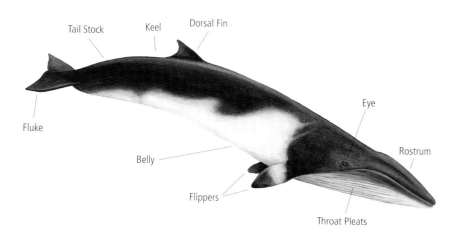

Tail Stock   Keel   Dorsal Fin

Fluke

Belly

Flippers

Throat Pleats

Eye

Rostrum

LARYNGEAL: referring to the larynx in the region of the throat, which can be made to vibrate to produce sound

LOB-TAIL: a display in which a whale forcefully slaps its tail flukes on the water's surface

MELON: an ovoid-shaped fatty organ found in the forehead of all toothed whales and believed to be used in echolocation

MIGRATION: the journey that an animal undertakes to get from one region to another, usually in response to seasonal and reproductive cycles

MYSTICETE: any cetacean that has baleen instead of teeth

NOMADIC: referring to creatures that move from region to region solely in response to food availability and that otherwise do not migrate

ODONTOCETE: any cetacean that has teeth instead of baleen

PINNIPED: a carnivorous, aquatic mammal of the suborder Pinnipedia (order Carnivora) with a streamlined body specialized for swimming and limbs modified into flippers (e.g., seals, sea lions, walruses)

PLANKTON: the tiny plants (phytoplankton) and animals (zooplankton) that drift in the water column and are the base of the food chain

POD: a small herd or school of whales

PORPOISE: *v.* a method of moving through the water that involves alternately rising above the water's surface and then diving underwater

PUP: a baby pinniped

ROOKERY: a colony of breeding animals

RORQUAL: strictly used, a whale in the genus *Balaenoptera*; most authorities also include the Humpback Whale

ROSTRUM: the forward-projecting snout of a cetacean

SONAR: the ability to detect or track objects underwater by monitoring their sound emissions or how sound bounces off them

SPY-HOP: a whale behaviour in which the animal, while in an almost vertical position, raises its head out of the water just far enough to look around

STRANDING: an event where one or more cetaceans come onto land or into shallow water and become stuck

TERRITORY: a defended area within an animal's home range

THREATENED: likely to become endangered if limiting factors are not reversed

TUBERCLE: a small, rounded nodule on an animal's skin

VENTRAL: pertaining to the belly (compare **DORSAL**)

VESTIGIAL: a part or organ of a creature that has atrophied or is rendered functionless by the process of evolution

VULNERABLE: refers to a species that is of special concern because of characteristics that make it particularly sensitive to human activities or natural events

Further Information

Emergency Hotlines for Atlantic Canada

Department of Fisheries and Oceans
1-800-565-1633
www.nfl.dfo-mpo.gc.ca
www.mar.dfo-mpo.gc.ca

**Marine Mammal Stranding Network,
c/o Yarmouth SPCA**
Nova Scotia
902-742-9767

Marine Animal Response Society
Nova Scotia
1-866-567-6277

Local Contacts and Research & Conservation Groups

Cetacean Science at Dalhousie University
Nova Scotia
whitelab.biology.dal.ca

Canadian Whale Institute
New Brunswick Field Office
506-752-1985
www.canadianwhales.org

**Grand Manan Whale and Seabird
Research Station**
New Brunswick
www.gmwsrs.org

Whale Release and Strandings
Newfoundland and Labrador
www.newfoundlandwhales.net

Atlantic Whales
Newfoundland
www.atlanticwhales.com

Online Information

American Cetacean Society
www.acsonline.org

Cetacea
www.cetacea.org

**Convention on International Trade in
Endangered Species of Wild Fauna and
Flora (CITES)**
www.cites.org

Dolphin Research Center
www.dolphins.org

The Dolphin Institute
www.dolphin-institute.org

International Marine Mammal Project
www.earthisland.org/immp/index.html

Ocean Link
oceanlink.island.net/oinfo/oinfo.html

Project Aware (Aquatic World Awareness, Responsibility and Education)
www.projectaware.org

Seal Conservation Society
www.pinnipeds.org/index.php

Shedd Aquarium
www.sheddaquarium.org

Whale and Dolphin Conservation Society
www.wdcs-na.org

WhaleNet
whale.wheelock.edu

Whales on the Net
www.whales.org.au

Further Reading

Boschung, H.T., Jr., J.D. Williams, D.W. Gotshall, D.K Caldwell, and M.C. Caldwell. 1983. *The Audubon Society Field Guide to North American Fishes, Whales and Dolphins.* Alfred A. Knopf, New York.

Bulloch, D.K. 1993. *The Whale-watcher's Handbook: A Guide to the Whales, Dolphins and Porpoises of North America.* Lyons & Burford, New York.

Carwardine, M. 1995. *Whales, Dolphins and Porpoises.* Dorling Kindersley, London.

Carwardine, M., E. Hoyt, R.E. Fordyce and P. Gill. 1998. *Whales, Dolphins & Porpoises.* Nature Company: Time-Life Books, Alexandria, Virginia.

Clapham, P. 1997. *Whales of the World.* Voyageur Press, Stillwater, Minnesota.

Conner, R.C., and D.M. Peterson. 1994. *The Lives of Whales and Dolphins.* Henry Holt and Company, New York.

Corrigan, P. 1991. *Where the Whales Are: Your Guide to Whale-watching Trips in North America.* The Globe Pequot Press, Chester, Connecticut.

Darling, J.D., C. Nicklin, K.S. Norris, H. Whitehead and B. Würsig. 1995. *Whales, Dolphins and Porpoises.* National Geographic Society, Washington, D.C.

Gordon, D.G., and C. Flaherty. 1990. *The American Cetacean Society Field Guide to the Orca.* Sasquatch Books, Seattle.

Kraus, S.D., and R.M. Rolland. 2007. *The Urban Whale: North Atlantic Right Whales at the Crossroads.* President and Fellows of Harvard College. USA.

Mason, A. 1999. *Whales, Dolphins & Porpoises.* Altitude Publishing, Canmore, Alberta.

Reader's Digest. 1997. *Whales, Dolphins and Porpoises.* Reader's Digest Explores Science & Nature Series. The Reader's Digest Association, Pleasantville, New York.

Rollins, D. and E. Byrd. 1995. "The Hello Dolphin Project." First International Symposium on Dolphin Assisted Therapy, Sept 8–10, Cancun Mexico, Proceedings: 17.

Stewart, F., ed. 1995. *The Presence of Whales: Contemporary Writings on the Whale.* Alaska Northwest Books, Anchorage.

Stonehouse, B. 1998. *A Visual Introduction to Whales, Dolphins and Porpoises.* Checkmark Books, New York.

Index

Page numbers in **boldface** type refer to the primary species account.

About the Author

TAMARA EDER, equipped from the age of six with a canoe, a dip net and a notepad, grew up in Alberta with a fascination for nature and the diversity of life. She has a degree in environmental conservation sciences, and has photographed and written about wildlife in Bermuda, the Galapagos Islands, the Amazon Basin, Argentina, Tibet and India. With a fondness for paleontology, Tamara has studied and participated in paleo digs in Alberta and Patagonia. She has worked in both Canada and Argentina as an interpretive naturalist and guide, specializing in ecology and paleontology. An award-winning photographer, her photographs appear in numerous books, posters and online magazines. Tamara now lives in Patagonia, and she continues to write, photograph and travel.

About the Illustrator

IAN SHELDON has been captivated by creatures large and small since the age of three. Born in Canada, Ian later lived in South Africa, England and Singapore. Exposure to nature from so many different places enhanced his desire to study it further, and he earned an award from the Zoological Society of London and a degree from Cambridge University. He has also completed a Master's degree in Ecotourism Development. Ian is an accomplished artist whose diverse works have been shown in San Francisco, New York, across Canada and in England. He has illustrated or authored over 30 books, many of them bestsellers.